THE REWARD
OF WORSHIP

THE REWARD
OF WORSHIP

The Joy of Fellowship with a Personal God

Jack Hayford

Chosen
Grand Rapids, Michigan

Published by Chosen Books
A division of Baker Publishing Group
P.O. Box 6287, Grand Rapids, MI 49516-6287
www.chosenbooks.com

Paperback edition published 2007
ISBN 10: 0-8007-9148-4
ISBN 978-0-8007-9148-7

Previously published under the title *Manifest Presence: Expecting a Visitation of God's Grace Through Worship*

Published in cooperation with Sovereign World Ltd.

Printed in the United States of America

Library of Congress Cataloging-in-Publication Data for the hardcover edition is on file at the Library of Congress, Washington, D.C.

To You,
Lord Jesus Christ,
Who in grace and mercy have,
by the Holy Spirit
and
through the eternal Word
taught my soul to sing,
my heart to obey
and my spirit to soar,
as song, strength and power
have been found
in worship
before You
at the right hand of
the Father's throne.

Come and Be King

Come and be King, come even now,
Now as we sing, here as we bow,
Come and be King, Jesus be Lord,
Here as You're praised and adored.
   See every heart open to You,
   Uplifted hands now inviting.
Jesus be King here in this place,
Come now and rule by Your grace.

Hear as we pray, "Your Kingdom come,"
Singing we say, "Your will be done."
Come and be King, conquering sin,
Jesus we welcome You in.
   Cleanse every heart with holy fire.
   Let tongues of flame rest upon us.
Jesus be King here in this place,
Come now and rule by Your grace.

Glory to God, Father of Love,
Praise to His Son, reigning above.
Spirit of truth, thanks be to Thee,
Worship we God, One in Three.
   Almighty One, O Holy Lord,
   There is no god like unto thee.
Jesus be King here in this place,
Come now and rule by Your grace.

O how we yearn, come back again,
Jesus return, Savior of men.
Tho' we rejoice now in Your power,
Longing we pray for that hour.
   Trumpets will sound, clouds roll away,
   Then every eye shall behold You.
Until that day, ever will sing,
Lord Jesus, come and be King.

                                 J.W.H.

CONTENTS

ACKNOWLEDGMENTS

Every published author is a debtor, and it is not entirely equitable that so great a debt be discharged in such brief an exercise as adding a page like this one to the work. However, those who are so patient as to grace and enable, edit, publish and distribute a writer's work are gracious as well as remarkably capable. To these I am indebted—and with deep gratitude to God for each I want to say:

...My special thanksgiving is due Jane Campbell, Editorial Director of Chosen Books, for her understanding and assistance in enabling me to have the time and latitude I felt necessary to treat this work with the full measure of attention I felt constrained to give it. Jane, I know that worked considerable inconvenience for you and your team. Your graciousness was not only an encouraging boost to me as I navigated a most unusual schedule of unexpected demands, but your diligence—redoubling last-minute efforts to keep things on schedule—was yet another tribute to your servant heartedness as a leader in Christian publishing.

...A tribute of honor is due Tim Pettingale and Ann McMath Weinheimer. There is no way in the world that this project could have arrived from the distance it traveled without your dedication to a most demanding task. You took a set of 24 teaching tapes, uncoordinated for the purposes of becoming a single treatise, and evolved a highly readable manuscript—an achievement that opened the way for me to be able to move forward credibly toward a hopefully worthy book.

…Selimah Nemoy, my personal editor on so many projects, and the chief editor of all our publications at The King's College and Seminary, traveled more than an "extra mile" in helping me finish this work. In arriving at what I believe is a truly valuable and timely addition to my other writings on the subject of worship, Selimah's grasp of the spiritual principles involved assured arrival at my highest goal. I hope readers find the book what we labored toward it becoming, i.e., more than merely a "message." Our objective was to present what we trust the Holy Spirit may use to become *a mind-transforming, life-changing, leader-influencing, worship-life-enlarging volume* for each reader.

Finally, and as always,

…You, my dear Anna, are more of this book than anyone else, for you have walked and grown with me for a half century, not only in our marriage and ministry, but in our learning and living a life of worship. Without you I cannot imagine the possibility of having experienced what we have—so abundant a life, which has constantly been broadened in joy and fruitfulness, as our precious Lord has flowed *His* life to us and through us, as we have followed His call and as we have daily bowed at His throne.

Jack W. Hayford

INTRODUCTION

A Shake-Up at the Showdown

I turned in my seat, as my flight for London's Heathrow neared England's shores, and saw the shaft of early morning light coming through the jet's window across the aisle from me. To my surprise, in the airplane cabin's orange-red glow, I saw a man huddled on the floor.

Most of the other passengers were still sleeping; we had flown all night, having taken off from New York at about midnight the evening before. Yet I was awake, and as I glanced around, I was impressed to now see *two* men in the dawning light of the plane's cabin—the one kneeling on the floor and another man standing several paces away, as though he represented something of a counterpart to him.

The man on the floor was clearly Arab in appearance and Muslim by practice, a fact that was abundantly evident as he knelt upon a prayer rug he'd spread in an apparent effort at aligning his worship as closely toward Mecca as his sense of direction in flight would allow. He bowed repeatedly— forehead to the carpet—compelled by his conviction that wherever he was, worship was mandated of him.

The man standing nearby had on a yarmulke, one of those small skullcaps worn by Orthodox and Conservative

Jews, especially when at worship. His long, sideburn curls indicated his Hasidic background. As he quietly but fixedly mouthed the words from his opened prayer book, his head bobbed backward and forward in rhythm and with a pattern revealing marked intensity. Worship was no option for this man either.

Both men were totally focused on the being each of them honored as God.

I begin the pages of this book on worship by noting this airborne encounter for two reasons: (1) the timeliness I feel in its release at this season of history, and (2) the test I feel the Church—and all believers in Jesus Christ, her Lord—face at this same juncture. Our times are those that "try men's souls"; and our testing as believers is in what will determine whether our worship prevails at this season in history or not.

We are at what is unquestionably the most decisive moment in history, at least to date. It is a time when everything is being shaken. That shaking is occurring across the gamut of human experience—from world governments to world economies as well as the world's environment. Events of catastrophic proportion are not the exception today; they are the norm. And in this era of gargantuan conflict between cultures, politics, armies, ideologies and within nature itself, it is not a stretch to believe that we may be seeing at least the prelude to the last great shake-up. There is such a one described in God's Word:

> See that you do not refuse Him who speaks ... whose voice then shook the earth; but now He has promised, saying, "Yet once more I shake not only the earth, but also heaven."
>
> Hebrews 12:25–26

Those words are sobering on any terms, and whether we are nearing history's climax, or simply experiencing another of its radical times of cataclysmic change, there is counsel for us in the following verses:

> Therefore, since we are receiving a kingdom which cannot be shaken, let us have grace, by which we may serve [worship] *God acceptably with reverence and godly fear. For our God is a consuming fire.* Hebrews 12:28–29, emphasis added

Inescapably present, in the text above, as well as in the actions of the two men I witnessed on that airplane, there is a dominant fact: Worship is central. And as the Hebrews passage says, it is exactly *that* to which we are pointedly called at such a time—that "we may serve God"—that is, *to worship Him.* We are summoned to worship with such a dimensional reverence and sensitivity to His glorious presence and power that a new dimension of responsiveness transforms us. *Such a transformation via worship is an absolute necessity for each believer and each congregation who seeks to serve God's Son, Jesus, today.*

Worship is changing in the Church. For at least two-thirds of my fifty years in pastoral ministry, I've observed—and participated broadly—in an evolving awareness and renewal of worship. It has penetrated liturgies with new life and shattered traditions with oft-disconcerting challenges to human preconceptions. It has brought vitality and freshness to many, while at the same time, on occasion, has introduced "space" for distortion, confusion and faulty definition of what worship's renewal is actually about. What *is* today's worship awakening about? Well...

It isn't about music.
It isn't about becoming "contemporary."

It isn't about cultural awareness.
It isn't about being "cool," "hip" or "with it."
It isn't about misty-eyed intimacy with God.
It isn't about theological accuracy *about* God. But . . .

It's about the formation of hearts in the presence of
    God.
It's about the shaping of disciples who know Him
    through being with Him.
It's about the transforming work the Holy Spirit
    achieves when pure worship occurs.
And it's about preparation for the last battle.

Those two men, unfortunately, represent something of a
drastic confrontation shaping up today—a confrontation
between the age-long struggle between the laws of God and
the lawlessness of man. They also dramatically demonstrate
to us that in the final analysis, worship plays into the
outcome of the struggle. Furthermore, they each manifest
convictions about worship, a consistency at worship and a
boldness in worship that exceeds the average Christian.
Even for many of us who *do* worship, convictions, consistency and boldness are a mixed bag. There is a frightening
reality to that fact that does not bode well for the Church
unless the reformation of worship advances to deeper levels
in our hearts, our homes and our churches.

A simple example of our Christian slowness to commit
to worship is seen in how *both* men on the airplane so
unashamedly gave themselves to worship. This is not only
notable in their heartfelt exercise that "awakens the dawn"
with worship, but how their convictions were fixed—that
the worship of their God calls for more than thoughts
about worship or the withholding of its expression until

either could get in a formal gathering with others at a mosque or synagogue. They worshiped where they were when dedicating their day to their deity, and they worshiped with manifest passion—unabashedly bowing or bobbing, each with a bold display of his (respective) prayer rug or prayer book.

This isn't the average Christian's style. We have been lulled by notions of "grace" that refuse to let the Holy Spirit teach us life-giving principles, *laws* if you will, of worship. And one wonders to what degree the zeal manifest by each of these men, multiplied by the millions who believe as they do, explains the spiritual dynamic that is presently manifest in each of their traditions. On the one hand, witness the alarming spread of Islam across the earth, and on the other, the raw power of survival that sustains a globally beleaguered Jewish community.

In the middle of it all, we are moving toward a showdown. This present reality is summed up in those two men, and it faces us with questions we can neither theologize away nor pretend will dissipate like mists on a lovely morning. We need to ask ourselves:

- Will the Gospel of Christ be advanced, or will it be forced to retreat in this day, as the anti-Christ spirit driving global Islam gains momentum?
- Will the existence of Israel and global Jewry face another holocaust at this season when worldwide anti-Semitism is on the rise and Christians are being called to take a position either for or against Israel?

Whether you or I even like to ask these questions, or even if your notions of history preclude the possibility of negative answers to them, I pose them for a very practical reason bearing on this book: I believe worship determines outcomes.

I'm persuaded that these points of showdown are only a part (but a very important part) of the reason the Holy Spirit is seeking to bring about a second shake-up. Besides the cluster of national and international issues shaking our world, He is at work—seeking to glorify Christ in, among, through and beyond the living Church. He is calling those who will "hear what the Spirit is saying to the churches" to ever-deepening dimensions of grasp and grace; to grasp a real understanding of worship, and to open to the grace that releases the power of worship.

To answer that call is to move toward a quest for God—for Him, as well as His power; for His manifest presence *now*, as well as His glory *forever and ever, amen.* Such a quest will neutralize our capacity to be either hypnotized by our own traditions, or satisfied with our present presuppositions. And none of us is immune to the threat of imagining that we have worship figured out. Even in offering what follows in this book, I run the risk of being thought of as supposing I am among the handful who "really know worship." But I don't suppose that; I only know that I have been a life-long learner (who is still learning), and I offer within these pages a bit of what it is that I've gained.

So with that, let me conclude with a maxim that, as a sixteen year-old, I heard my pastor say and which I wrote in the back of my Bible—knowing I was called not only to Christ but also to serve His Church:

> God is not so interested in what we are,
> as He is in what we are becoming.

Thus, "for such a time as this" I offer this resource to you. May my words help both of us to "follow on to know the

Lord"; to know Him all the more through worship, and to glow Him all the more in a world that, beyond its shaking, is seeking. The dynamism of the Church in answering to the heart-hungry quest of the multitudes will always distill to our worship as a people—and to whether, amid our worship, seekers discover the manifest presence of the One True and Living God—Father of our Lord Jesus Christ.

In His Name, still a "becoming" child,
Jack W. Hayford

PART 1

THE CALL TO WORSHIP

Worship Christ the Risen King

(To tune of "Angels from the Realms of Glory")

Rise, O Church, and lift your voices,
   Christ has conquered death and hell.
Sing as all the earth rejoices;
   Resurrection anthems swell.
Come and worship, come and worship,
   Worship Christ, the Risen King.

See the tomb where death had laid Him,
   Empty now, its mouth declares:
"Death and I could not contain Him,
   For the Throne of Life He shares."
Come and worship, come and worship,
   Worship Christ, the Risen King.

Hear the earth protest and tremble,
   See the stone removed with pow'r;
All hell's minions may assemble
   But cannot withstand His hour.
He has conquered, He has conquered,
   Christ the Lord, the Risen King.

Doubt may lift its head to murmur,
   Scoffers mock and sinners jeer;
But the truth proclaims a wonder
   Thoughtful hearts receive with cheer.
He is risen, He is risen,
   Now receive the Risen King!

We acclaim your life, O Jesus,
   Now we sing your victory;
Sin or hell may seek to seize us
   But your conquest keeps us free.
Stand in triumph, stand in triumph,
   Worship Christ, the Risen King!

                           J.W.H.

Manifest Presence

The Living God—"Waiting in the Wings"

When I stepped onto the platform I was warmly greeted by about five hundred leaders—mostly young singers, musicians and others involved in providing leadership for their congregations' worship. Their average age was in the 25- to 30-year-old bracket; their bright countenances and expectant faces were enough to encourage any speaker. This was about the tenth time I had addressed such a setting in the past two years, and I was accustomed to both—the anticipative excitement of the group as well as their embracing acceptance. I was enjoying the privilege of partnership with Integrity Music's Seminars for Worship, and another opening plenary session was about to begin.

As you and I open these pages together, I feel very much the same thing. We are partnered in a joint inquiry—a quest to pursue the potential that the Holy Spirit's global awakening to worship is affording us as the living Church advances into the 21st century.

- *His* is the call to worship: The Holy Spirit wants to help us glorify Christ.
- *His* is the directive to approach God's throne: There is the fountainhead of power.
- *He* is the Author of our manual for worship: God's Word awaits our study.

Indeed, the Holy Spirit is summoning believers *every-where*; the whole *world* is being touched with a sense of the Spirit's moving us to bow, to pray, to lift our voices, to exalt the Name of Jesus—to worship the Living God. But why? What is the Holy Spirit up to? I say this because there has *never* been a time that it has not been appropriate, desirable and important that humankind worship God. There is *never* a moment that it would not be worthy for individual believers to pause, fall to their knees, lift their hands in humility and praise and thank God for His daily mercies as well as His priceless gift of salvation's grace through our Lord Jesus Christ, His Son.

So *why now*—why at this season in the Church's history is *worship* becoming the watchword of the moment? Why are thousands of young leaders—often joined with their pastors—sacrificing two full days of their usual schedule to come to seminars for one purpose: to deepen their understanding of and focus their gifts solely on the worship of the Most High God, Creator of all things and Giver of Eternal Life in Christ?

I am persuaded the answer is pure and simple: God almighty is stirring hearts to worship because He is about

to make an entrance. Because worship is pivotal to His being welcomed into earthly settings and situations, His Spirit is moving His people to, as it were, "roll out the red carpet—the King is coming to visit you."

Let me be clear: I am not making reference to the ultimate entrance of the King, not intending to define this "coming" as that moment of consummate glory and power when the Son of God will come with a shout and the voice of the last trumpet—the Second Coming of Jesus Christ. But I am speaking more immediately and specifically to God's readiness and desire to enter the arena of human circumstance—to manifest Himself in glory and spiritual power, *today*. As the primary Person bringing a redemptive scenario into reality where you and I live, God is waiting in the wings—and worship is the invitation to which He responds.

To be even more specific, let me assure you—this is happening already. I am fully aware, and you may be, too, that there are hosts of worshiping believers who have already established vital habits of passion and holy patterns of worship, worship to which God has already responded. Yes, even as we traverse these pages, worship is paving the way for waves of divine grace to flow at thousands of locations and in millions of hearts. So while God *is waiting* to make an entrance where millions of others are (indeed, *billions!*) He is also *working*—making *entrances* (plural). He is invading circumstances, moving in power, demonstrating His grace, revealing His sovereign might, extending His Kingdom mercies and transforming people, churches, communities and whole regions of the earth. And the common denominator of these visitations of divine entrance is that clouds of praise to His name have preceded the rain of His blessing—of His arrival in power.

THE MANIFEST PRESENCE

To speak of a "divine entrance" can easily create concern among some cautious souls. My selection of words, however, is both biblical and intentional, and it is important from the beginning of my "conversation" here with you, dear reader, that you understand my frame of reference. In the preceding paragraph, I used a series of phrases to describe cases and places where God is working in ways that (a) are clearly beyond human ability to produce what is taking place, (b) are sequentially parallel to or pursuant to a commitment of otherwise ordinary people to worship Him in humility and with passion, and (c) bring more than momentary or transient results in individual lives or collective human circumstances. In short, there is something *manifest*—God's hand at work in inescapably evidential ways.

I have learned that there are entire sectors among the vast body of Church leadership who are troubled by the two-part notion that (1) God is waiting for a human invitation to manifest Himself, and (2) worship is the means for inviting Him to do so. And I understand their difficulty, because to their view I am suggesting that God is either weakened or passive apart from human worship or instigation of His actions. But that is not at all the proposition as it appears in Scripture, nor as it is applied by understanding worshipers today.

Perhaps you have heard detractors of today's worship revival decry the idea that "worship invites and makes way for the Kingdom of God," usually mocking or assailing that proposition with accusations that such an idea is to propose that God can be manipulated. The opposite, of course, is true. God is God—an obvious reality, but an eternally glorious and unchangeable fact. He is almighty over all, glorious beyond words, wise beyond thought and loving beyond measure. But as grand and true as those facts are, He is also patient beyond understanding, and His dealings with humankind are flavored by a self-imposed insistence that He await the welcome of human hearts who consciously decide they want Him in their lives.

Free will is not paradoxical to God's sovereign will in the divine economy of things. The latter insists on the former— God's will, in the realm of earth's affairs and human circumstances, is that humans *respond* to the reality of His love and power by issued invitation. Without that, He limits the fuller revelation of His glory and power to them. It is precisely that principle that sets the foundational truths undergirding our expectation that prayer is meaningful—that it makes a difference. As it said on the aged plaque on my Sunday school classroom wall when I was a boy, Prayer Changes Things.

By Jesus' own instructive pattern for prayer, we are taught that worship is the steppingstone into the presence of God. He tells us, "Pray this way!" (see Matthew 6:9–13):

1. Come, knowing you have a relationship with the Creator who made you: "Our Father in heaven, . . . "
2. Worship, acknowledging the exceeding glory of His holiness and wonder: "Hallowed be Your name."
3. Invite His activity into your world—asking for heaven's best into earth's need: "Your kingdom come. Your will be done on earth as it is in heaven."

All that proceeds from that point has been predicated on worship that invokes God's will and works. The principle of worship as decisive is put in place here, if nowhere else.

Of course, this is not the only place where the role of weak and sinful humanity is placed in so decisive a position regarding our potential of realizing the almighty power and grace workings of the eternal God. The Bible is packed with instances that reveal the profundity of God's divine patience—that He has chosen to make humankind His partner in any way. And the Word also reveals God's readiness to work mightily when human hearts align with His throne and thereby invite, invoke or welcome His presence. As, for example, Ephesians 3:20–21 balances the matter:

> Now to Him who is able to do exceedingly abundantly above all that we ask or think, according to the power that works in us, to Him be glory in the church by Christ Jesus to all generations, forever and ever. Amen.

In these oft-quoted words, please notice how often they acknowledge the dynamic relationship between worship and God's workings, although this relationship is too seldom understood. Notice:

1. The exceeding *ability* is God's—"to Him who is able." He is like a mighty river seeking a riverbed through which to flow. However:
2. The measure of the *power* released is determined by redeemed humans—"according to the power that works in us." In short, the mightiness is God's, and the avenue of that power awaits human openness.
3. The worship and *glory* belong to God—"to Him be glory in the church." It is not incidental that the principle is no sooner stated (see verse 20) than the pathway is pursued (see verse 21). Early believers understood the relationship between their worship and the release of God's power into their lives, congregations, world.

To make such an observation is neither to dignify man beyond biblical proportion nor to dethrone God or reduce Him to a place of an unscriptural dependence upon man. But the revelation of Scripture does have defined limits as to what God will impose or allow without human consent or choice. And when His redeemed, who have made their choice for His Son, the Savior, choose to learn His ways and walk in pathways of worship, He seems very willing to respond with "exceedingly abundantly" more than they could imagine.

Worship brings ever deepening and expanding dimensions of God-at-work in our world. Worship, in a very real sense of the word, opens a doorway to the power of His presence, confounding dark powers and overthrowing sin's destructive operations. In Paul's words of expressed spiritual warfare, worship and praise exalt God and cast down those facts and forces that seek to exalt themselves above Him (see 2 Corinthians 10:3–5). Essentially, it is God's presence—the raw dynamic of His Being and Person stepping into a setting—that gives place to His transforming, redeeming, delivering power.

I have learned, however, that there are theologians of a certain stripe who take issue with this proposition. "Worship brings His presence?" they say with critical inquiry. "Why," they continue, "God is present whether you or I ask Him to be or not!" And the exclamation mark becomes a sharp assault on the notion that worship makes any difference in God's presence being revealed in our world or in that dimension. To clarify, and to dismantle the crippling doubt such resistance sometimes prompts in believers' hearts, let me define what I mean in using that word—*presence*.

AWESOME, ABIDING AND AMAZING

The Bible reveals at least three different dimensions by which God makes His presence known. Indeed, He *is* everywhere. But the ways He chooses to manifest Himself imply certain distinctions. Consider: God's awesome presence, God's abiding presence and God's amazing presence.

God's Awesome Presence

The word *awesome* is a contemporary adaptation of the older word *awful*—a word that meant "filled with awe" (that is, awe-full), not "something horribly bad" as the word has come to be used today. It was commonly used in reference to our ultimate accountability before God; being required finally to answer to Him on "that dreadful and awful day of the Lord"; to face up to the "frightening implications of standing before the awful presence of the eternal God."

This is a feature of God's presence that has paled in the wake of the theological dumbing down of the Church over recent years, not to mention the erosion of the fear of God amid the pride-filled vanity present in so much of our society. The psalmist cries, "Where can I flee from your presence?" The answer is given: *Nowhere! You're everywhere!* (see Psalm 139). Hebrews 4:13 says of God: "All things are naked and open to the eyes of Him to whom we must give account."

This feature is a humbling reality, which is summarized in the Word of God to indicate:

1. God is omnipresent and all-seeing.
2. God is just and takes into account all we say and do.

3. We will each give an account for those words and deeds.

Together, these facts call us to worship God with reverence and to walk softly before Him, relating to others with love, justice and good works.

God's Abiding Presence

There is a second dimension of God's revealed ways of relating to us; it is in the tenderness, understanding and warmth of a personal relationship. When repentance for sin and faith in Jesus brings us back to the Father, the Savior describes an entirely richer dimension of God's presence: "He who has My commandments and keeps them, it is he who loves Me. And he who loves Me will be loved by My Father, and I will love him and manifest Myself to him" (John 14:21).

This is a distinct level of relationship with God, deepened by such promises as "I will never leave you nor forsake you" (Hebrews 13:5), and "Lo, I am with you always" (Matthew 28:20). It is an invitation to worship God in a way that brings about a personal intimacy—a nearness and dearness like that expressed in the old hymn: "He walks with me and He talks with me, and He tells me I am His own."

The flow of truth regarding God's presence moves forward from the *objective reality* of God's awesome *omnipresence*, which relates to all humankind, to the *subjective relationship* of God's abiding *personal presence*, by which He relates to all His redeemed. From this, the truth flows toward the possibilities inherent in those expressions of God's mightiness—mightiness that awaits those who

worship Him and call upon Him to manifest His presence in
their midst or into certain situations.

God's Amazing Presence

Such a call and invitation as these possibilities include are
evidenced in God's Word. The early believers called for
God's manifest presence, saying:

> "Lord, You are God, who made heaven and earth and the
> sea, and all that is in them.... Now, Lord, look on their
> threats, and grant to Your servants that with all boldness
> they may speak Your word, by stretching out Your hand to
> heal, and that signs and wonders may be done through the
> name of Your holy Servant Jesus." And when they had
> prayed, the place where they were assembled together was
> shaken; and they were all filled with the Holy Spirit, and
> they spoke the word of God with boldness.
>
> Acts 4:24, 29–31

Isaiah cries out for God's power-filled, demonstrative
workings as well:

> Oh, that You would rend the heavens!
> That You would come down!
> That the mountains might shake at your presence . . .
> To make Your name known to Your adversaries,
> That the nations may tremble at Your presence!
>
> Isaiah 64:1–2

These are not shallow requests for a dramatic event
sought by sensation seekers. These are worshipers declaring, "Lord, You are God, Creator.... Lord, make Your name
known." They have come before the throne of God, not
for their own entertainment or for reasons of human vin-
dictiveness. And their worship, applied with such a bold

summons for God's almighty intervention, is instructive to us for it gives evidence for the fact that worship may proceed from the *reverent* to the *intimate*, and then to the place of *welcoming*—indeed, *calling* upon God for a dynamic manifestation of His presence and His power.

THEIR "CALLING" SUMMONS OURS

The boldness of these worshipers, with similar cases throughout the Bible, still meets with hesitation among some who see worship as only meditative or devotional—as only designed to honor and adore the Lord—or who only enjoy quiet fellowship with Him. The idea of worship as a means of partnering with God and welcoming His power is too seldom understood. Thus, the Church at large tends to be resistant to worshiping God with the expectation of His visiting with power. But the model seen in that early Church worship service incorporates a summons to us:

- Worship is more than an objective exercise, worthily extolling His glory; and
- Worship is more than a devotional exercise, intimately pursuing His fellowship; but,
- Worship is also a biblical means of entering into a role of partnership with God's almightiness.

It is that possibility that compels a quest for every dimension of God's manifest presence.

Living worship will touch hearts with God's presence as the omnipresent One—drawing them to answer to that internal sense of accountability that inescapably gnaws at honest souls. Living worship pursues relationship with

God, too; longing to know His Person, to walk with Him in intimacy, to simply be with Him—to be more interested in the personal presence of God than in even the greatest display of His power. But joined to these great possibilities within the manifest presence of God, living worship is being stirred by the Holy Spirit today, awakening the living Church to *all* the dimensions of divine breakthrough that worship may discover.

At this hour in which the Spirit is calling God's people into His presence with a new sense of expectation, what preparation of heart, soul and mind might each of us need to best respond to Him? Having issued His invitation to us, He is, dear one, waiting in the wings for our worship—ready to step center stage, not only into our midst to manifest Himself, but also into our world to disclose a freshness of His power and glory through a Church aflame with His love.

CHAPTER 2

The Spirit's Crescendo of Worship

The Invitation to Worship

> After these things I looked, and behold, a door standing open in heaven. And the first voice which I heard was like a trumpet speaking with me, saying, "Come up here, and I will show you things which must take place after this." Immediately I was in the Spirit; and behold, a throne set in heaven, and One sat on the throne.
>
> Revelation 4:1–2

It is without question that among the Bible's most breathtaking scenes is the one described in Revelation 4–5, as we are ushered into the throne room of the universe! Consider with me John's words as he attempts to describe in the mundane resources of human language the transcendent splendor of heaven's glories, centering his attention where all sentient beings logically would—on the royal seat and personal glory of the Creator Himself.

The Almighty's appearance is vividly brilliant, like that of diamonds and deep red carnelian. A rainbow circles His throne "like an emerald," and amidst the incredible glory of the Lord, celestial beings are worshiping day and night, awestruck to the point of ceaselessly bowing down and rising up again to proclaim, "Holy, holy, holy, Lord God Almighty, who was and is and is to come!" (see Revelation 4:1–8).

A profound insight into the possible significance of the recurring actions of the cherubim (here referred to as "living creatures") was suggested to me years ago. David Stern, who since has done such remarkable scholarly work in producing a New Testament for Jewish readers, worshiped with us regularly prior to his moving to Jerusalem. One day, as different members of the congregation exchanged reflections on biblical texts that feature worship, David commented on what appears at first to be the creatures' repeated bowing at God's throne—as though possibly required by God and rendered in rote and submissive obedience.

While there is no question that God is worthy of all the honor, reverence and even abject adoration expressed by these creatures most approximate to His throne, David noted how God is most highly honored when any creature willingly and voluntarily brings its worship with verbal praise, presenting that worship with attendant physical expression.

"It seems to me," he said, "that these creatures are not simply exercising a habit as they 'rest not day or night, saying, "Holy, holy, holy, Lord God Almighty, who was and is and is to come!"' Rather, as they worship, bowing down each time only to rise and look again upon the face of God, their declaration explodes from having seen yet another facet of the glory of God's beauty and Person. Freshly overwhelmed at what they have just seen, they fall before Him again, only to rise up and capture another view of the wonder of who He is."

My soul resonates with that insight, which, I am persuaded, is at the heart of the ever-increasing crescendo of praise that springs from these beings and spreads relentlessly around God's throne—and wherever its revival or restoration is being embraced.

THE PROPHETIC PICTURE OF WORSHIP

Worship is the core value of the book of Revelation, whatever else is made of its prophetic pictures. No book of the Bible has had more written about it than this one, but too little notice has been made regarding the way it is laced through with scenes of worship. Beside, and quite frankly preceding, this book's place as a manual on "last things," Revelation is a book of intensely practical (not speculative) value, and at its fountainhead is its uniqueness as a source of understanding about worship:

- John falls before the glorified Christ in worship (see chapter 1).
- The Church is called to "hear what the Spirit is saying," as a worshipful response to the present "word" of Christ to His people (see chapters 2–3).
- Martyred souls gone before us into glory are heard calling from heaven's altar of worship to the Most High (see chapter 6).

- The Church, delivered from out of the great Tribulation, is heard extolling God and the Lamb before the throne (see chapter 7).
- The dynamic power residual in the cumulative worship (incense) and prayers (intercession) before the throne is witnessed as it prompts God's acts of judgment (see chapter 8).
- The contrast to worship that honors God is seen as the text reveals the destiny of destruction coming upon those who "worship demons and idols" (see chapter 9).
- Worship thunders from heaven as the last trumpet is sounded; worship appears to play a partnering role in God's economy, seeming to ignite a release on earth of those things ordained in heaven (see chapters 10–11).

These cover only the first half of this revealed "worship book"—text that introduces us to the awe-inspiring relationship between *our worship as His redeemed creatures* and *God's response of releasing His will on earth*. This is illustrated simply yet pointedly in chapters 4 and 5.

These two chapters are a single event, the text flowing as a continuum; a humanly imposed chapter division breaks them. As readers move through chapters 4 and 5 of Revelation, we are first "taken up" (4:1) and permitted to witness the spectacle that is God's throne of glory. The "Holy, holy, holy" of the living creatures becomes the first strains of what will be a progressing crescendo. It begins there and moves to the song of those who witness the arrival of the Lamb. Then, just as the Creator Father is extolled at the beginning of the text, the exaltation of the Redeemer's Son begins as those around the throne sing, "You are worthy . . . and have redeemed us to God by Your blood" (5:9).

Yet this is only the beginning. The Spirit's crescendo of worship is seen in ever-widening, concentric circles. As it begins first with one saint (John) "in the Spirit" and in the presence of God (see 4:2), it moves to worship exploding from the angelic beings closest to the throne of the Most High (see 4:8) and spreads outward to be chorused by a band of ruling elders surrounding God's throne (see 4:10–11). The theme that has been inaugurated in heaven is now amplified to include redemption's hopes for earth, now achieved through the blood of the Lamb, who is praised for His sacrifice and the magnificence of His wisdom, honor, strength, glory and blessing (see 5:1–12). But the dimensions of the crescendo are still only beginning.

An innumerable host of angels joins this worship, now revealed and being realized through the Lamb's sacrifice and victory. From this, the book of Revelation proclaims a procession of praise through the era yet unfolding, describing history's travail all the way to the eventual triumph of the Lamb as King of kings and Lord of lords. But in anticipation, verses 13–14 of chapter 5 project the scene even further in time—the worship becomes prophetic. It seems to move across time and around the world, extending in concentric circles, until we see a climaxing crescendo of praise by all of creation—those that are in the earth, on the earth, under the earth!

This process is essential to our grasping what really takes place in the fourth and fifth chapters of Revelation, as John steps in the spirit into the eternal realm—a realm that is not measured by the clock. It is likely that this prophetic glimpse involves more than we think at first glance. John is beholding worship at the throne of the Maker of all creation, but it is also entirely possible:

- that John is seeing creatures at worship almost immediately following earth's creation,
- that he is hearing praise to God moments following the majesty of the Almighty's spangling the heavens with the stars, and
- that what he describes of that consummate crescendo of worship yet to be realized is an extension of worship into which we are moving presently—as worship invades and drives back the darkness, making way for the advance of God's Kingdom into the eventual triumph of redemption's purposes.

The reason for examining this remarkable passage of worship's crescendo is that it can help us understand two important points: Not only is worship a constant throughout the ages, but also, its absence creates a barricade of resistance to the release of God's will and purpose. To see this at the beginning of our study will help us to understand:

- why worship so often becomes distorted, confused or trivialized—becoming a value that is lost to neglect, passivity, ignorance or formalized, soul-numbing rituals;
- why worship sometimes becomes a show—a performance taken over by once-sincere leaders who, like Lucifer, have become blind to the folly of preoccupation with their own achievement in leading worship;
- why worship is too seldom allowed to invade Church life and becomes packaged in ways that assure human control, rather than sensitive companionship with the Holy Spirit; and
- why worship, when it is embraced biblically in an incarnation of the truth of the Word (that is, not only

teaching about worship, but being filled with the Spirit of worship), is the key that will unlock healthy personal life and service for anyone, and release dynamic breakthroughs of evangelism and spiritual growth in any congregation.

Let's look further into the scenario this Revelation passage provides—the overwhelmingly grand and glorious worship around the throne of God that is revealed to John. And while not attempting an exhaustive study of the relationship between prophetic texts and worship, I think several other Scriptures can join to help us arrive at some practical and personally encouraging points. I believe this will provide you with a clearer understanding of the pivotal link between worship and the advance of Christ's Church and His Kingdom. It will also help you to see how worship in your life is vital if God's promises and purposes are going to be achieved in your relationships, pursuits, desires and challenges.

The living Church is God's means for advancing His redemptive purposes. Worship is at the core of that possibility.

GOD'S WILL BARRICADED

Looking at the scroll, John weeps because he recognizes that the will of God has been sealed and cannot be disclosed. He weeps because there is no one to open it.

> Then I saw a strong angel proclaiming with a loud voice, "Who is worthy to open the scroll and to loose its seals?" And no one in heaven or on the earth or under the earth was able to open the scroll, or to look at it. So I wept much,

because no one was found worthy to open and read the scroll, or to look at it.

Revelation 5:2–4

But then, an elder speaks: "Do not weep. Behold, the Lion of the tribe of Judah, the Root of David, has prevailed to open the scroll and to loose its seven seals" (verse 5).

It is not incidental that reference is made to the tribe of Judah in this scene: Not only did Judah's hosts lead the way in Israel's battles, but also that tribe's name means "praise"! The Lamb's lion-like powers are also linked to His being an offspring of David, who was not only Israel's most success-ful warrior but also history's most devoted and remembered singer of worship and praise to God.

Though the exalted Messiah is present as a mighty warrior, John describes Him as a sacrificial Lamb whose death has accomplished all that the Old Covenant required of worship. Arriving in heaven, bearing the fresh "marks of slaughter"—the "wounds that once had caused his death" (verse 6, NEB, TLB)—we are presented with the sole candi-date who can recover earth and humankind from ruin.

As I earlier noted, John is actually witnessing the full spectrum of all redemptive history, beginning with Jesus Christ's return to heaven at the time of His ascension, an event that occurred about fifty years before John's vision. Yet at the same time, he is used by the Holy Spirit to present us with a full spectrum of heaven's worship—from the creation of all things to the consummation of all things on this planet.

With the help of the Holy Spirit, John describes witnessing, in the presence of the Father, that moment when the Son of God, the Lamb—having been resurrected from the dead; having spent those days with the disciples and told them,

"Go into all the world and preach the Gospel to every creature"; having ascended into heaven following His farewell message on the Mount of Olives (see Acts 1:1–11)—now arrives in heaven, returning to the eternal glory, mission completed!

- *His presence* here, depicted and lauded as the victorious Lamb, shows us worship extending from that moment until the last trump is sounded and the ultimate triumph realized.
- *His presence* here declares that the price of salvation for humankind is paid in full, His provision for their justification and sanctification is secured.
- *His dominion* shown here over all powers of hell and every force of evil makes it possible for human vessels to be cleansed of their filth and sin and be filled with the Holy Spirit, so that He can commission a people for His purposes.

Jesus declares, "I will build My Church and the gates of hell shall not prevail against it" (see Matthew 16:18). He is now ascended before the Father—His mission to obtain salvation for humanity now achieved—"It is finished!" However, His mission to extend His victory throughout the earth, through the Body of the Church to which He has given birth, has just begun!

There is no mystery as to the reason John wept over the apparent unavailability of an adequate representative to take the scroll and break open its seals, nor for the reason all heaven rejoiced—as does John—when the Lamb appears and takes it from the Father's hand. The scroll as described is that exact kind of document that was prepared in that era of Roman history to serve as a person's will. This scroll, in the hand of God, represents His will for earth and human-kind—a scroll that became sealed and closed through the death of man who succumbed to sin, bequeathing a curse to earth rather than the blessing intended by the Creator's will (see Zechariah 5:1–4). This scroll, however, was retained in the hand of the Almighty until a worthy representative of humankind could legitimately release His will for earth and humankind anew and afresh. Through that release, the scrawling of the thief and the liar smeared on the scroll (see verse 3) could be overthrown—consumed by the power of the One who bears the Father's name.

This is the context for all the worship that follows. It is recognition of this that prompts those praising Jesus. I cannot press this point too strongly: *Heaven's crescendo of praise rises in the atmosphere of (a) a revealed, victorious Savior, and (b) a certain engagement of the ongoing struggle between the Truth and the liar, the Savior and the thief, the Living God and the evil one.*

This is the flow of the book of Revelation. This book, so often submitted to sincere speculation about the time of Christ's coming and a search for matching current events to Scripture, is actually targeting a much loftier and more certain theme. Whatever worth other studies of this work afford (and I mean no assault on any), our call—as individual believers and as the people of God today—is to hear the Holy Spirit's call.

It is a call to Spirit-filled worship.

It is a call to spiritual warfare.

It is a call to steadfast commitment *beyond* the paraphernalia and the excitement of a worship renewal—a call to the purpose, principles and power with which God Himself has invested the subject of worship. As we so often say, "It's all about Him!" And that's true.

But with Him, there is a wonderfully gracious, companioning truth: Worship is His gift for you, too. Obviously not *God* worshiping *man*, but God designing worship as a means for His beloved creatures to know Him, to enter into the abundance of His fulfilling and fruitful purpose for us, and to find the high delight of His realized will for us, in us and through us.

Continue with me . . . alongside John . . . and let us see his encounter with the practical goodness of God who meets us in our circumstances—who not only delights in our worship, but also delights in demonstrating His readiness to pour out blessing around us as we pour out our hearts in worship at His throne.

CHAPTER 3

The Joy of Worshiping a Personal God

The Reward of Worship

> I heard a voice, saying, "Come up here and I will show you things to come."
>
> Revelation 4:1, paraphrase

One of the most difficult things in the world is finding balance, especially when you have the challenge of putting great truths into proper perspective. It is amazing how the habits of sincere people often make us so intense and so entrenched in a *good* thing that we become peculiarly able to turn it into a *bad* thing. When that occurs, it is even more difficult to explain how any truth that relates to God Himself can possibly become cast in a negative light.

Throughout five decades of pastoral leadership I have had frequent occasion to deal with dear people who were passionate about something of God's truth and pursued its application with near vengeance. They focused their faith forcibly, pursuing a value the Bible revealed, yet the fire of their own human energy (sometimes interpreted as the fire of God's Spirit) became self-consuming and, at times, destructive to their relationships or personal ministries.

Worship is often distorted this way.

Later in this book, for example, we will discuss some of the challenges in liberating worship from formalism, without degenerating into formlessness. But for the moment I want to continue our look into the encounter John records in the book of Revelation, of His being "caught up" into the presence of God. The issue of imbalance upon which I would like us to focus can be posed in the words of this question: Was John "caught up" for the purpose of seeing God in order to worship *Him*? Or, did God bring John into His presence in order to help John understand how much God cared about *him*?

In seeking balance to the question, "Who is worship really about?," please understand that in no way do I want to detract anyone's attention from the truth of God's greatness, almightiness, worthiness and sovereign power. First and foremost, above and beyond all, *He is*. Period! That is why He revealed Himself to Moses as "I AM."

This "ever-present-ness" of God bespeaks more than the fact of His eternal nature and omnipresent Being. It summarizes the complete fullness, adequacy, perfection and beauty that characterize His Person. So whenever we discuss the subject of worship, it is understandable that the primary Person in view is the ultimate One. Worship is, as we have said, "all about Him."

There is another facet of God, however, that is also "all about Him." It is this: He not only *is*—ever and always—but in His own Word, the Bible, He wraps up everything that He is in one word. He says conclusively, in effect, "More than anything else, this is what I'm about: 'I AM *Love*.'"

With this statement—"God is Love"—God's Word has suddenly turned the tables on us. It is as though He is balancing something for us, as though He is saying: "You may come to worship Me. I welcome your appropriately bringing glory to Me because it is right. But it is also good for your own sake that you worship Me, not because I need your worship, but because through it, you will be progressively liberated from yourself (which is life's worst bondage). By worshiping Me, you are also being brought to a place of intimate relationship—one of knowing, understanding and walking with Me.

"As well," He might continue, "I want you to know where *My* focus is: My will, My interests, My power, My purposes, My commandments, plans and objectives are never about *Me*. They are about *you*. They are all targeted for *your* blessing, *your* fulfillment, *your* fruitfulness and *your* realizing My purpose in creating *you*. And the reason I have given *My* ways of worship to you is this: so that by those means *you* might 'Come up' from where you are, and enter into all I have for you."

A PICTURE OF TWO-EDGED TRUTH

God's desire for our worship is not wrapped in mystery. From Creation, worship—honoring God and His ways—was essential in order that life, productivity and ongoing joy-filled purpose might be realized. Worship has never lost that ultimate objective. As soon as sin entered the human scene, however, its intrusion via our broken trust with God introduced the necessity of a prerequisite. For worship, relationship and the blessing of fellowship with God to be reinstated—that is, for any of us to realize a return to the place where God could fulfill His original plan for our lives—worship had to become *redemptively* oriented. Instead of worship advancing God's *creative* purpose for our lives, worship now required sacrifice in order to neutralize the separating power of human sin and failure.

And sacrifice required rules. Fallen human understanding required commandments to renew human minds in those principles that would keep life from self-destructing. But while advancing His redemptive answer to human need, God had not forgotten His original intention. The goal of bringing each of us through the doorway of redemptive worship by drawing us back to Himself through His Son, Jesus, was always—and still is—one thing: to bring to our lives all the benevolence and benediction that our Loving Father God wanted us each to have in the first place. So through Christ, whose sinless life and perfect sacrifice answered for our sin-and-self-distanced relationship, two things occurred. Not only do we now have the opportunity to be forgiven and born-again into eternal life, but we also have been invited to walk into and continue in a relationship with the almighty God that increasingly discovers:

- how to see the unfolding of His purpose for us;
- how to grow unto maturity as reborn children of His;
- how to walk by faith when blindsided by life in a broken world;
- how to overcome the adversary of our souls; and

- how to rise above the "gravity" pull of our yet-tainted humanity.

Having looked together at the "crescendo of worship" that Revelation 4–5 initiates, let me invite you to return to that setting, to look at the same passage through another set of lenses. Having seen what we need to see of God, examine with me things in this text that indicate how He looks *for* us, looks *after* us and goes *ahead* of us. Take some time to meditate on how greatly God desires our worship—not for what *He* gets out of it, but for what *we* receive from it—what we can experience distilling around us of His abundant benefits and restored purpose for our lives.

Don't be afraid to take this kind of look into His Book. In fact, He desires for you to see the picture of His love for you; to see how present and powerful He wants to be in your behalf. Dear one, the picture is here.

PICTURE GOD'S LOVING WAYS

The book of Revelation will help us understand a lot more if we will submit to its remarkably prophetic nature, rather than trying to structure its events into a neat sequence on a chart of prophetic events. In saying that, I don't doubt there are some elements on every chart you have ever seen that have veracity and value. The difficulty, however, is that people become so tied to a system that they miss the simplicity and the beauty of what is being said.

Our focus here is to see a picture of God's loving ways in the context of the praise and worship setting into which John is summoned. It is here that God invites you and me to "Come up" to His presence, to move "in the Spirit" beyond our circumstances, to witness and to worship at His throne where await us a rainbow of promise and the certainty of His power.

John's Circumstance: A Trumpet Call to Transcend

In Revelation 4, John says he heard "a voice... like a trumpet" (verse 1). He is making reference to a voice he has heard before, the voice of the Savior (see Revelation 1). John is hearing Jesus summon him into the presence of the Father, into the presence of heaven. This stepping into the eternal realm constitutes a transcendent moment: " 'Come up here, and I will show you things which must take place after this.' Immediately I was in the Spirit... " (Revelation 4:1–2).

It was not transcendent in the sense of being an escape from reality—John is being summoned *beyond the limits of where he is*. For us to come in the spirit of worship and seek the face of the Lord is a response to the same invitation. But why is it issued by a voice like a trumpet? Why is Jesus calling John with a shocking shout and not a still, small voice? Consider John's situation; perhaps you are in same place.

There are two things true of John right then: First, he is in a state of personal confinement by reason of his incarceration on Patmos. Persecuted by the Romans, John is restricted from being able to do what he wants to do. And second, he has just received word from Jesus Himself that five of the seven churches that are under his oversight are in pretty sorry shape. Jesus commended every church, but there were enough things wrong for Him to say, in essence,

"I have somewhat against you.... Let's get this corrected" (see Revelation 2–3).

The door of opportunity for John to make any difference in the Church has been slammed shut by Rome. He is probably eighty years of age by this time and could easily be thinking, *I'll never make it out of here.*

Here is a picture of every one of us at some time or another, finding ourselves at a point of despair, wondering whether or not we will ever move beyond what restricts us, feeling that God could not possibly be pleased with us as His servants. It is a mix of concern we have over the things that have us trapped as well as concern regarding our ability to serve others in a genuinely Christlike manner. For John, the limits were the boundaries of an island. For us, it may be an island of circumstance, or perhaps distance and isolation in a marriage.

Suddenly, the voice calls to John: "Come up here...." It summons him beyond those restrictive, limiting—even imprisoning—circumstances through an open door to God's throne room where John is about to see Jesus in a way he has never seen Him before. He is about to have a revelation of Jesus' ultimate triumph beyond everything else.

Immediately, the text says, he moves "in the Spirit" into an eternal moment that is both transcendent and teaching—it is the scene of worship where he captures a sense of God's promise (the rainbow) and His power (His throne), of the triumphant Lion and the redeeming Lamb.

Through the Open Door: A Vision of Victory

Three things take place as John steps through the open door. First, he says, "I saw a throne." He is speaking about the Most High God. He is saying that he has been brought to a reminder that everything he deals with—as problematic as it may be—is trivial by comparison with the grandeur and the glory of that throne. That does not mean God regards my circumstance as trivial in His heart. He knows I am dust; He knows those things are significant to me, but He is greater. He is grander. He is above it. *I saw a throne.*

Second, John sees those who are worshiping around the throne. And they are worshiping the One who is the Creator. This is not only the One who rules above all, this is the One who is able to take nothing and bring about anything that is needed. In other words, you never need believe that you have reached the dead-end for hope. The worst situation we can be in is the place where we declare that there is nothing that can be done. If you find yourself there, remember that God is your Father and call home. Better yet, come home. Step through the open door. It is here, worshiping at the throne of God where He is able to refill us with His Spirit, renew us with His hope, reassure us with His love and revive the dreams and desires He has given us from disappointment and despair.

Third, there is a reason for that rainbow around the throne. The rainbow is not just pretty; it is the reminder of a promise that extends beyond everything that looks as though it is ruined and will never be restored. By the sign of the rainbow, God spoke to Noah about the catastrophic flood that befell the earth, telling him: "That's never going to happen again." So many people live through the terror that the bad things that have happened in the past are going to happen again. There are some who have been battered and scarred by circumstance, and the Lord says, "Step in, look at the throne, see the Creator who is able, and the rainbow of promise for you."

It is here that John receives the restorative blessing of reminder that Father God has all creative power and is able to bring anything into being. In this magnificent scene of splendor, majesty and worship that surrounds the throne of God, John is reassured that despite the circumstances of exile and imprisonment he is enduring on earth, there is never a hopeless situation with God. This is a picture of God's open-door policy, of the Almighty's loving ways toward you and me.

Jesus calls His people to a transcendent moment, which is found in our worship of the Living God. The message that cycles over and over again in the book of Revelation is that while the world will always seek to limit and oppose you, and while Satan will always confront you with the ferocity that only hell can muster—beyond it all, Jesus is Lord and He dwells in you. In Him we have the ultimate victory and that victory may be applied here and now by our worship.

The beginning point is recognizing that He sees us where we are and summons us beyond that to "Come up here!" We are invited to step through the open door and draw near to Father God so that something may transpire in us—to come and encounter Him in ways that engender the deepest workings of His Spirit in our lives and prepare us for the next stage of what He wants to do through us. Not only are we called to be people who know how to be renewed in worship, but also the overflow of our worship can draw others into the river.

It is not just John's experience; I believe it relates uniquely and pointedly to many of us. It was significant to "the churches," and not only those that John oversaw. While the letters went to the seven churches, the whole message is "to the churches." That means it is for you and me, right here, right now. It is related to the Church's life in every era, but uniquely to the Church's life, I believe, in the last era. When will that be? I have no notion; none of us does. From the time that I was a boy, I believed Jesus was going to come very soon. I still do. That is not generated in me by some kind of hype. I believe the revived Church has always believed that Jesus was coming in this present generation. And it will be true as we come to the last generation. Somebody once asked me, "Do you believe that this is the last generation?" and I said, "I don't know, but it sure is ours."

There is a responsibility to live in this "last generation" motif anyway, as David served God in his generation. Ours is our last. Why does the Church always think it is the end? I believe it is because when we are in the spirit of worship, revival and renewal we are quickened to the proximity of His presence. Jesus is moving vitally in our midst right now, so we sense He must be ready to step through the door. That is why the revived Church always believes that Jesus' coming is in our generation.

The life of the Church of Jesus Christ is going to have an impact on our world multiplied more times than it presently does—and not only when it is awakened to the joys, the blessing and the vibrancy of living worship. This is a reality that has begun expanding in the Church for the last two decades, and one, I believe, the Holy Spirit is seeking to advance.

Our review of the Savior's summons in this passage of Scripture reinforces our awareness of the dynamic awaiting us personally. Worship is not only the worthiest exercise for humankind to reach its potential, it is also the most fruitful and the most practical. John's answer to that call opens a new awareness of God's power, presence and ability to transform his situation from one of need to adequacy. So in that light, it is your call—your invitation to answer His call.

God's Word reveals how readily He will loose what has been sealed against His will—in your life, your family, your community or any other part of your private world. That is what happens when worship says, "Let Your Kingdom come and Your will be done . . . in my world, as it is in Yours, Father God."

So let me invite you. Simply say: "Jesus, I come with gratitude. Thank You for the hope of Your help as I step through the door that is open to me—my doorway into the presence of the Father. Thank You for the confidence that His creative power and Your redemptive ability are able to deal with whatever obstacles are confronting me right now."

Then, begin to participate in the crescendo of worship. And keep praising.

CHAPTER 4

Worth Its Weight
in Glory

The Substance of Worship

Arise, shine;
For your light has come!
And the glory of the LORD is risen upon you.

Isaiah 60:1

There is a distinct beauty to the word *glory*. It communicates by its very use a rainbow's variety of splendid applications—from the radiance of a bride walking down a church aisle on her wedding day, to the triumph of an Olympic athlete being crowned with a laurel wreath and decorated with a gold medal as that nation's anthem resounds around the world. We associate the word with achievement or excellence, and understandably so. But the idea inherent in *glory* has to do with something more—the "something" with which a person, thing or practice is invested that marks its superiority or excellence over other persons, things or practices.

The Old Testament includes a poignant story of a child's birth and his mother's death, which both occurred simultaneously with their nation's defeat and embarrassment. It is a touching tale nestled at the heart of Israel's earliest history as a people at the time they were struggling to find their identity as a nation. It was during this quest for securing their place in the land of promise that we learn a lesson from the emphasis the Bible puts upon the relationship between the worship of God and a person or people's victory or defeat in battle.

Just as with all historical incidents in the Scriptures, the purpose in God's Word is not simply to record the past. It is to reveal timeless principles that show how life may be lived in fruitfulness, or how it may be pursued unwisely and result in failure. The inextricable link between worship and the abiding presence of glory is seen in the story—a lesson indelibly fixed before us as a message from heaven. It teaches: "You can't fool around with Father God—at least not if you want to win at life."

It is because Israel's historic quest is parallel to all human endeavor—our lifelong pursuit of fulfillment, purpose and meaning—that this link between "glory" (experiencing excellence in life) and "worship" (relating to the One who is the giver of life) is so essential to our understanding. It distills most simply in a succession of statements illustrated in the story of Ichabod: Worship in a person or group's life determines worth, worth determines weight, weight determines value and value secures glory.

There are four pieces to the tale.

1. The time was one of confusion, where impurity had polluted the worship practices of the spiritual leadership among God's people. Eli, the high priest, is negligent. His preoccupation with his own interests, shown by piggish indulgence on the sacrifices brought by Israel's worshipers, manifests in self-inflicted obesity. Eli is a study in worship gone self-centered.

2. At the same time, Eli's sons—supposedly the heirs to spiritual leadership in the land—were living an aggressively immoral lifestyle. Honoring God could not have been further from their minds. Their corrupt ways stand as an ancient case study of that same corrosive behavior that sometimes is excused among spiritual leaders today. Eli's sons are a study in worship gone worldly, the perennial threat to the health of the Church today, wherever leaders are excused for immorality or other unworthy behavior as long as they "keep the show going."

3. Into this sordid hour came a series of attacks against the Jews, launched by the Philistines who, like today's militant advocates of Jihad, were relentless in their resistance to Israel. The response of the Israeli military was based not on historical precedent—but on a beautiful reality that had now become only an empty tradition. They asked Eli if they could take the Ark of the Covenant into battle, believing that—as in Moses' and Joshua's day—the *presence of God* would attend their quest for victory and enable their triumph. The Ark was not only a symbol of God's presence but also a prompt for obedient worship. But for them, the Ark was nothing more than a good-luck charm—a kind of rabbit's foot carried in the hope of God's blessing and power. Worship was absent, relationship with God was unknown and religious forms had supplanted spiritual understanding. The result? They lost the battle, of course—a message that speaks all the way to

our day: Worship without spiritual substance is nothing more than superstition. Accordingly, it will gain nothing of God's blessing and end in everything of confusion.

4. Finally, it was when the report of their defeat in battle unfolded that a series of further tragedies struck. Not only had thirty thousand Israeli men been killed (including Eli's sons), but also the Ark of the Covenant had been captured by the Philistines. Eli, shocked by the report, fell over backward, broke his neck and died. His daughter-in-law—hearing of her husband's death in battle—went into premature labor and died as her baby was born. Her last words reflected that moment in Israel's history—the defeat of the day, the loss of family members and the capture of the Ark—as she named the child *Ichabod*, meaning, "the glory has departed." The story consummates in a description of the impact upon people and nations when worship becomes empty of spirit and void of truth, and the weight of glory is reduced to a vapor of toxic incense distilling from worship emptied of meaning.

THE TRUE VALUE OF WORSHIP

The ancient English word for "worship" is *weorthscipe*, which incorporated the idea of "ascribed worth." It meant fundamentally that a true worship of God is more than an exercise of religious ritual; it is a human expression of a proper value being placed on the Person being worshiped and the personal cost of the practice of worshiping Him.

True worship takes place when we declare the Lord's worth:

- when we come before Him to honor His character, not parade our music or ministry talent;

- when we come before Him with humility, not protecting ourselves from the penetrating power of His
  Spirit; and
- when we open as children to the truth of His Word,
  rather than smugly defending our narrow-minded,
  doctrinaire attitudes that produce more division than
  unity in Christ's Body.

We most honor the God who created us and the Lord
Jesus who redeemed us when we ascribe the right value to
Him. He is *worth* our praise, adoration and exaltation. Such
worship is designed by Him—directed by the principles in
His Word to enable and release the entry of His glory and
the unfolding of His strength, substance, joy and liberty
in our lives. It works the transformation described in
2 Corinthians 3:17–18:

> Now the Lord is the Spirit; and where the Spirit of the Lord
> is, there is liberty. But we all, with unveiled face, beholding
> as in a mirror the glory of the Lord, are being transformed
> into the same image from glory to glory, just as by the Spirit
> of the Lord.

The weight of His glory, exalted in worshiping the Father
and magnifying His Son in the power of the Holy Spirit,
impacts, reshapes and alters our character and conduct. It
liberates, releases and loosens us from the hold of sin and
self and unleashes the ministry-life of Jesus Christ to course
through our daily lives. "From glory to glory" is the Word's
description of a life being progressively transformed to walk
in the fellowship and blessings that were always God's
intent for us.

Worshiping Him who is *worthy* assures worship that will
issue in *glory.*

It is that truth that brings us back to Ichabod—to the name that means "no glory."

Chabod is the Hebrew word for "glory," and its deepest meaning lies in the fact it most commonly refers to weight, weightiness, substance. (The "I" in *I-chabod* is a prefix that negates the "weight of glory"—hence, the "departed glory" that the name lamented.) And it is here that this story summons us, by contrast not comparison, to be warned of the things that remove true worship from the heart. It invites us to review the things God is looking for when we worship—the qualities that bring the *chabod* of His presence into direct encounter with our lives, shaping them and investing them with the weight, substance, blessing and presence of His glory.

It expresses the entirety of the Bible's progressive revelation of God's effort to recover and restore lost glory to humankind. What was lost through violated fellowship and forgotten worship in the Garden of Eden is confronted there by God Himself. His sacrifice of the creature that brought a re-clothing of the fallen pair is a picture of worship that re*covers* and renews the possibilities of His original intention for every man and woman to be restored.

As worshiping congregations or as worshiping individuals, we need to be renewed regularly in our perception of God's purpose in calling us to worship. Otherwise, we are just as vulnerable as Eli, his sons and the people of Israel to fall prey to the empty habits of form (however faithfully we perform them) or our undiscerned surrender. Like Eli and his sons we might find ourselves in the midst of a God-setting, yet yield to an indulgence of ourselves rather than be shaped by His transforming Spirit.

It merits asking to what degree this truth has yet to penetrate every corner of the Church. To what degree have believers been mistakenly taught that worship is merely the warm-up for the sermon, or allowed it to become a joyless, religious obligation? How often does mere excitement substitute for a depth of hunger for God, or does a fanatic abandon to good sense replace spiritual genuineness and a discernment of God's desire for our full-hearted worship? In that regard, to what degree do self- and pride-preserving hesitation obstruct believers from joyously expressing praise before God?

In contrast to the potential for disappointing answers being found to those questions, consider what may happen as you and I—as an awakened Church—open ourselves to the Holy Spirit's conviction, correction, refocusing and refreshing regarding worship. *The transformation brought about by the weight of God's glory will leave the mark of His presence on all of us!* That cannot help but evoke a "Hallelujah!" from anyone who knows God's love, who wants to exalt His Son and who will say, "Holy Spirit, come upon me and bring this about!"

My personal feeling is that an increasing portion of the global Church is moving in that direction. I have seen it in the faces of tens of thousands in conferences and congregations. I have read of it where hearts are opening and heaven comes to fill those who "hunger and thirst after righteousness."

I also found evidence of a renewed quest for what God wants in our worship in today's Church when I received a phone call from the editor of one of evangelical Christianity's most respected magazines for church leaders.

"Jack," he said, "we're doing a complete issue on worship and want to ask you to contribute an article for it." I affirmed my availability if he felt I could serve their objectives in that issue, and was surprised to hear what he said next. "We certainly don't believe that good theology alone is the key to answering God's expectations for our worship. I know you would agree that knowing the Word and grounding in God's truth is important, but in discussing this forthcoming issue of the magazine our editorial team agreed: *The tendency of evangelical Christianity is to study truth about worship, rather than to open totally to God as we worship.*" He went on to request that I address the question, "How do we 'get to the heart of worship'?," and asked me specifically, "Will you write an assessment of God's expectations of our worship as you see them and as you apply them?"

So turn the page with me, and let me share what I wrote. My conviction is that it cuts to the quick of those issues that will keep *weight* in worship and assure God's *glory* being manifest by His presence among His people and in our churches.

CHAPTER 5

In Spirit and in Truth

Getting to the Heart of Worship

"But the hour is coming, and now is, when the true worshipers will worship the Father in spirit and truth; for the Father is seeking such to worship Him."

John 4:23

People sometimes ask, More than defining what we think worship should be like, what kind of worship is God actually looking for? It is a worthy question, and while the Word of God clearly calls us to worship in truth as well as in spirit, all the theological textbooks and presuppositions in the world cannot substitute for what we most need. That is why it is worth examining what can happen to any of us when we decide simply to prostrate our pride, open our hearts and let His Spirit begin to shape a childlike spirit in us, bringing us to a practical and genuine broken-unto-true-humility hunger and thirst for God.

Even though I have practiced, led, studied and preached about "worshiping God" for over five decades as a Christian leader, I still refuse to suggest I have any expertise on the subject. A lifetime of entering and experiencing His presence has a way of keeping me mindful of how little I know, and how dependent I am on *Him*—not on my experience— for today's guidance in leadership.

The matter at hand for us is, What type of worship honors God? Or, to look at the question another way: What is it, after all, theologically speaking, that actually makes worship worshipful to God?

I open with that context for what follows—my offered answer to the above pair of questions presented to me— with the request: "Set forth the theological basis for our thematic study of worship."

At first a certain reticence tempted me to conform to what I supposed was expected—a treatise on the glory of God and the propriety of humankind bringing worthy expressions of worship before His throne. Of course, His grandeur and greatness *does* recommend our humble and our highest expression of praise, as well as our utmost in devotion and adoration, but I felt the need to get to "the heart" of worship. So I have chosen to press an issue—not less theologically correct, to my view, but one that might seem unacceptable for failing to parrot the usual when a "theology of worship" is proposed.

To my perception, most theological presuppositions about worship focus on the cerebral, not the visceral—on the mind, not the heart. In most Western Christian traditions, a virtual scorning of either the subjective experience or the mystical nature of encountering God finds common approval. A usual theology of worship centers on an objective analysis of God's revealed Person, nature and attributes, with the accompanying presupposition that worthy worship essentially constitutes our reciting this information back to Him. This focus on the mind's ideas *about* God, rather than the heart's hunger *for* Him, overlooks the truth that worship is actually a gift from God to us, more than one of ours to Him; that He is more interested in helping us than we are capable of interpreting Him. Our Western, evangelical tradition often seems a schoolish insistence that worship is an intellectual exercise. But the words of our Savior still resound the undeniable call to worship that transcends the intellect: "God is Spirit, and those who worship Him must worship in spirit and truth" (John 4:24).

We have been inclined to conclude that "mind" and "spirit" are synonyms, when the Bible shows us that the "heart" is a more likely candidate to answer to the meaning of "worshiping in *spirit*." The fact that "in truth" is a companion phrase, indicating the active participation of the intellect as well, is undeniable; but it is also inescapably second—and dependent upon the heart's fullest release in worship *first*.

This priority is usually held suspect, if not resisted outright, because our intellectualized value system minimizes the worth of emotions. The heart, as the more emotionally motivated center of our human response, is deemed less worthy for being governed more by affections than by reason; it is seen as more vulnerable to deception than the intellect. But to turn on this basis, from heart-begotten (that is, "spiritual") worship to an intellectually based approach, is to entertain a dual delusion: first, that the mind is less subject to deception than the heart (an unsupportable concept; see 2 Corinthians 4:4); and second, that the mind is *ever* means by which God is contacted in worship (which is denied in the Bible; see Job 11:7).

This is not to denigrate the priceless value of God's gift of human intellect, nor to deny that human intelligence is contributive to worship. But our quest is to answer, "What kind of worship does God prefer from us?," and honesty with the limits of any human being's brainpower forces the issue. In the last analysis, His Word indicates that He is not looking for something *brilliant*, but something *broken*: "The sacrifices of God are a broken spirit, a broken and a contrite heart—these, O God, You will not despise" (Psalm 51:17). It is not that our minds are unworthy vehicles to receive divine *revelation*, but that they are too limited to respond to the divine *invitation*. The intellect may discover truth about God's worthiness of worship and may chose to worship. But to enter fully into the dimensions of our Creator-Redeemer's presence—to open to the intimacy to which He invites us, as well as to that ecstasy with which eternal love desires to enthrall the human soul—only the spiritual capacities of the worshiping heart will suffice. The exercises of our enlightened minds may *deduce* God, but only our ignited hearts can *delight* Him—and, in turn, experience His desire to delight *us*!

That is His desire, without question. God's invitation to eternal life and eternal joy is an expression of His preoccupying concern from the inception of His ideas about and creation of humankind. Our fathers have taught us this: "The chief end of man is to love God and to enjoy Him forever" (Westminster Catechism). This anticipated joy is not reserved solely for the future life, for Peter says of our present worship of Christ, "whom having not seen you love. Though now you do not see Him, yet believing, you rejoice with joy inexpressible and full of glory, receiving the end of your faith" (1 Peter 1:8–9).

So, I would contend that what is on God's mind when we worship Him is not how many grandiose thoughts we have about Him, but how passionately our hearts desire Him; and that what He most wants to achieve in the intercourse of our spirits with His is the transmission of love, life and joy. Thus, I tread the risky territory of seeming to minimize worship by not focusing first on "God's holiness and our unworthiness"; by proposing that, from God's viewpoint, worship is a means designed to unlock the human heart that He may answer to human need and serve His own heartfelt interest in the well-being of His most beloved creatures. I also hasten to emphasize, of course, that God's excellent glory and man's sin and need are not in question: He *is* holy and we *are* unworthy. But once the redemption provided through Jesus' cross has been received by faith, I want to assert:

- that the worship God most welcomes is neither essentially nor primarily intellectual (though it is certainly not unintelligent); and
- that God's primary focus in giving us access to worship Him is to provide an exposure and experience intended for *our* benefit, not His (though it is unquestionable He delights in our coming to Him).

I propose such a theology of worship upon the evidence of His pleasure with worship offered to Him in settings reported in His Word, as well as in direct statements He has made. These reveal that the worship God welcomes and honors is:

- worship that treasures His presence;
- worship that humbles the heart;
- worship that sacrifices and expects something from God; and
- worship that extends God's love by every means.

Let's look at the evidence for these points.

Worship That Treasures His Presence

Foremost, God welcomes those into His presence who want *Him*. Their quest may be one of desperation or of delight, of frantic need or of a loving hunger for fellowship, but the motivation is clearly focused—and so is His pleasure with it.

In Exodus 33–34, a tender and powerful exchange takes place between God and Moses. It spans the range of actions from an intimate face-to-face encounter to a dramatic declaration by the Almighty, at which time the second set of tablets containing the Law is given to Moses. Central to this scene is the heart-cry Moses utters:

> "Now therefore, I pray, if I have found grace in Your sight, show me now Your way, that I may know You and that I may find grace in Your sight...." And [God] said, "My Presence will go with you, and I will give you rest." Then he said to Him, "If Your Presence does not go with us, do not bring us up from here." Exodus 33:13–15

Shortly following this, God displays His glory to Moses— as sure a sign of His pleasure and presence as He ever gives (see Exodus 40:33–38; 1 Kings 8:8–11).

It was not until I had been in pastoral leadership for nearly fifteen years that a transformation took place in my thinking about our corporate worship services. Rather than regiment our gatherings with concern over the aesthetics, mechanics and academics of our time together, we began to make a priority of including a non-pressured portion of the service for free-flowing songs of praise and adoration—often, songs directly expressive of the Scriptures. To this day, I usually introduce this time during our worship with brief instruction and notation of our objective—perhaps expressed as well as possible in the words of Graham Kendrick's musical setting of Paul's words in Philippians 3:7–11: "Knowing You, Jesus."

Within two years of our earnest quest for God's manifest presence among us—a season rich with its own fulfillment, and never void of a sense of His nearness—our church was visited with a display of His glory and grace that continues still. This continuance has not been without our periodic need for re-renewal in our own passion for Him. We are vigilant of the fact that even the finest spiritual habits are vulnerable to the arthritis of ritualism—when form loses its focus, though its practice may remain flawless in exercise. But with gentleness, the Holy Spirit has a way of drawing us back to "first love"—by regularly prompting renewed *hunger and thirst* for the Living God.

Such worship will be awed by His presence and fall in love with His Person. If the phrase "fall in love" seems offensive to anyone (as it once did to me, seeming not to be sufficiently objective), then perhaps we might learn to be offended by whatever line of reason distances the heart from a passion simply to know and love God.

WORSHIP THAT
HUMBLES THE HEART

Perhaps the most memorable encounter between God and any of the prophets is the occasion of Isaiah's call (see Isaiah 6:1–8). The abject cry of a sinful man, "Woe is me, for I am undone," was *not* an achievement of intellectual analysis, but of self-discovery upon entering God's presence with unabashed passion and with childlike openness. "I saw the Lord," he says with neither apology nor arrogance, as a breakthrough of grace produces a break-up of pride—a viewpoint even more deeply affirmed later in the same book (see Isaiah 57:15).

The starting place for confronting pride is in how we approach worship. Isaiah, who is known to be from the cultural, educated elite of Judah of his time, describes a childlike humility and teachability that can only attend an unpretentious entry into God's presence. His cry, without a vestige of style-consciousness and revealing an unreserved availability to God's revelation of Himself, is the very thing to which Jesus calls us all:

> "Assuredly, I say to you, unless you are converted and become as little children, you will by no means enter the kingdom of heaven.... Take heed that you do not despise one of these little ones, for I say to you that in heaven their angels always see the face of My Father who is in heaven."
>
> Matthew 18:3, 10

It is this heartfelt conviction of the essential need for childlikeness (not child*ish*ness) in worship that caused me to begin to understand why the Scriptures call us to *expressive* worship—both vocally and physically expressed—

verbalized without foolishness, dramatized without pretense. Few things challenge our pride more than the simplest summons to expressiveness (even to "sing a bit louder on the next second verse"). I carry no brief for orchestrated calisthenics in church, as though a set of exercises verifies a superior liturgical practice in God's eyes. But I have learned that careful teaching and pastoral modeling can help a congregation past the self-consciousness that releases a childlike liberty in expression ... and challenges our adult preoccupation with our own self-importance.

I think the motive was sincere, but it was misguided that day one of our members suggested I temper my pastoral practice in leading worship: "Pastor, if you didn't teach and invite people to lift their hands in worship, I think our church would grow faster...." The person then added, "I think you might injure some people's pride."

Without previous thought, my candid answer cut to the point as I see it: "Injure pride?" I said gently. "Why, I was hoping to kill it altogether."

I hold no disdain for the propriety of respecting human dignity. But there is a disposition, ensconced in the Church as surely as in the world, that equates dignity and pride—and it is a false equation. The worth of each individual in my congregation requires that I teach, help and model a pathway for all of us to "come as children before the Father." But the deceptiveness of pride, and its insistence on finding a way to justify its preservation—even in Church!—calls me to find a means to help hearts toward a humility like Isaiah's, one that will give place to a fresh view of God, and pave the way to deeply felt confession and purification in His presence.

WORSHIP THAT SACRIFICES
AND THEN EXPECTS

Hebrews 11:6 puts it clearly: "He who comes to God must believe that He is, and that He is a rewarder of those who diligently seek Him." The text is based on the proposition that worship always brings a sacrifice to God—that "he that comes," whether with praise, an offering or in the laying down of something being asked by the Holy Spirit's call, is *presenting something of him or herself to Him.* Yet simultaneously, we are told that the worshiper is, with equal faith, to believe something will be given in return by God Himself—something rewarding, enriching, benevolent and good.

The tension between these two—bringing a sacrifice and expecting a reward—provides a venue to common argument. Some feel obligated to defend God against human selfishness and would refuse the balance in proposition that the text declares. But the truth is, God *does* freely offer the rewards of His blessing—and delights to do so. He does not bother to argue: "Don't you dare give Me something and suppose you're manipulating Me to give back!" Instead, His Word simply says, in effect, "Since you believe in and come to Me, I would expect you to believe I will reward your quest." *Of course* tithes or offerings (which are, indeed, appropriate and biblical "sacrifices") are not to be a tit-for-tat bargain with God! But God's call to worship is attended by His own commitment to bless *us.* That is why I unhesitatingly teach the promises of God regarding His desire to bless us with physical and material provisions.

Whatever interpretive view a leader takes toward Malachi 3:10–12, quoted below, whether it is viewed as a contemporary covenant or not, it still reveals a largesse in the heart of God toward human obedience in giving—and the justice of human expectancy of blessing in conjunction with that obedient worship.

> "Bring all the tithes into the storehouse,
> That there may be food in My house,
> And try Me now in this,"
> Says the LORD of hosts,
> "If I will not open for you the windows of heaven
> And pour out for you such blessing
> That there will not be room enough to receive it.
> And I will rebuke the devourer for your sakes,
> So that he will not destroy the fruit of your ground,
> Nor shall the vine fail to bear fruit for you in the field,"
> Says the LORD of hosts;
> "And all nations will call you blessed,
> For you will be a delightful land,"
> Says the LORD of hosts.

It is not unspiritual to rehearse again the timeless fact: Worship is God's gift to us for our blessing and benefit. He does not need it. We do. And as we learn to enter with full and open hearts, we will find humbled and cleansed hearts, and ultimately come with full and opened hands that give ... and go away with His promise to refill them, over and over!

Those hands will learn one more thing.

WORSHIP THAT EXTENDS GOD'S LOVE

If indeed God-pleasing worship addresses human need more than it supplies divine need (if, indeed, there is such a thing as a need on God's part), it is to be expected that worship that honors the desires of the Almighty will beget *reaching* hands. It is, thus, unsurprising that our Savior's summary definition of the "greatest commandment" issues into "the second, which is like (in importance) unto it." The vertical mandate, which focuses on our worshiping God ("You shall love the Lord your God with all your heart, soul, mind and strength"), issues in the horizontal ("... and your neighbor as yourself"). Basically, the only truly divine approval our worship will find is when it results in hearts being focused on such things as:

- forgiveness toward others, with peacemaking and reconciling efforts evident in our day-to-day agenda for living;
- gracious, lifestyle evangelism characterizing our conduct and communication, so that the glory found in His presence is manifest in our shedding a warm, attractive "light" and a believable, winsome witness; and
- unselfish, servant-minded availability to assist in human need—seen in a heart of care for victims of neglect and injustice, nourished by a merciful mind-set toward those whose cheapened values reveal their blindness.

It is this conviction that drives an inclusion of prayer circles in nearly every worship service at our church. "Ministry Time" is the formal name we use for an approximately ten-minute segment of small-group interaction and prayer, usually following an extended time of sensitive, intimate and praiseful worship to God. The habit was formed decades ago at the same time that my thinking about worship was being revolutionized. The four to five minutes during which three to six people share their personal needs or concerns and then pray for one another, is an inestimable key to our effectiveness as a congregation.

Notwithstanding the doubts of those who wonder if such a practice might violate a seeker-sensitive style, we have found that Ministry Time:

- applies in pragmatic ways the sense of God's love evoked during the intimacy of worship;
- realizes the release of the ministry gifts of the Holy Spirit in the assembly;
- opens the doorway to personal expression, mutual concern and the power of pointed, heartfelt prayers with their consequent answers; and
- lays the foundation for the invitation at the end of the message (because it is infinitely easier to invite people to receive the love of God in Jesus Christ after they have had a personal encounter with some people who have shown it!).

Over the years, the bottom line of worship seems to have been and continues to be served as we pursue these values on the basis of the theological viewpoint I have presented. We have never lost sight of Him as first and foremost, but we have not based our approach on anything more than the splendor of His love shown to us in Jesus—and that love-gift ignites our worship. What begins in treasuring Him, proceeds to humble our hearts, awaken our sacrifice and release our service. What is birthed in the heart finds expression in the hands—hands that rise in humble praise, give in simple expectancy and serve with gentle grace.

With such sacrifices, God seems to be well pleased.

The summary of those four points, though brief, has seemed to congeal in my mind "what God is looking for in our worship," and over the years, I have found that three results distill continually and constantly as we apply them:

1. The congregation has experienced a profound constancy of a sense of God's presence in our midst. This manifests in a joyous reverence—not only in regard for the Holy One, but also in a liberating freedom in praise, rejoicing in the grace of Him who visits and moves among us as we worship.

2. We have avoided confusion regarding priorities and purpose. The classic quote "The main thing is to keep the main thing the main thing" is far easier to realize in a congregation where the pastors, elders, singers and musicians commit to worship as the first priority. And it must be realized in all of those groups—no relegating the congregation's worship ministry to a "music department thing." When that unified commitment to worship is made, everything else will fall into place, without power struggles, without competition and with a fluidity of all parties' gifts being actuated with wisdom and anointing. Business as well as program, fellowship as well as stewardship will all be flowing together.

3. We have experienced abounding growth in the personal lives of believers and expanding growth as evangelism reaches outward through the ministry of the Body. Growth in the Word of God and development as ministering people who penetrate the marketplace become a natural dissemination of the salt-and-light influence of the Church. Worship works! Its dynamic flows from heaven as God touches the world through people who have been in touch with Him.

These are our discoveries as we seek to grow in worship and realize the Father's fullest release and purpose in bringing us to Himself. Seeking to get to the heart of worship has shown us that, at the core of God's objective in calling His people to worship, there is not merely a divine summons to principles, but that we also revere, learn of and obey Him. This full-orbed worship after God's heart not only will fulfill principles but also will fulfill God's purposes as His power is released to and through His people. Thus, what begins in treasuring Him proceeds to humble our hearts, awaken our sacrifice and release our service. And what is birthed *in the heart* finds expression *in the hands*. As those hands are raised—giving expression to hearts that are lifted in humble praise—they are taught in His presence to give with obedient simplicity and to serve with gentle grace.

Having focused on these facets of God's purpose for our worship, let's proceed to an even more basic place of understanding and practice in worshiping God. Come with me to worship's "center point."

CHAPTER 6

Worshiping Him Who Is Worthy

The Person We Worship

> God, who at various times and in various ways spoke in time past to the fathers by the prophets, has in these last days spoken to us by His Son, whom He has appointed heir of all things, through whom also He made the worlds; who being the brightness of His glory and the express image of His person, and upholding all things by the word of His power, when He had by Himself purged our sins, sat down at the right hand of the Majesty on high.
>
> Hebrews 1:1–3

It is almost unimaginable to most 21st-century followers of Jesus to think that for three-fourths of the history of the Church, believers had no copy of the Bible. Even following Gutenberg's development of movable type, it was more than two centuries before sizable portions of the population could afford a Bible. Yet for all those centuries, the Church worshiped, the Person of Christ was exalted and the testimony of salvation through His cross was maintained. It is because New Testament worship had a center point—the Lord's table.

The accessible, readily available and mobile resource of bread and wine—established by the Lord of the Church Himself as the foundational ritual His people would observe—has, inherent in its elementary simplicity, a threefold cluster of worship essentials that, to this day, make His table a universal gathering place and a uniform point of worship.

Opinions differ as to what transpires at Christ's table. There are different requirements for accessing it. And there are several terms used to title its observance: Communion, Eucharist, Mass and so forth. But notwithstanding whatever differences, doctrines or dogmas may divide, the Lord's table has prevailed through the centuries as the center point of worship. This is true for one reason: It features the central Person and central proclamation of His Gospel.

Some Protestant traditions have placed the pulpit center-stage in their churches, but even in those settings you will find that the platform arrangement has a table (more often than not, either in front of or behind the pulpit) and almost always at the center! We worship Christ, but He is the Christ of the cross. With Paul we announce, "God forbid that I should glory, save in the cross of our Lord Jesus Christ, by whom the world is crucified unto me, and I unto the world" (Galatians 6:14, KJV).

To describe the heart of New Testament worship, we might diagram it thus:

The Central Person	The Center Point	The Center Piece
The Son of God	The Gospel of God	The Word of God
Jesus Christ	The Lord's Table	The Bible
Lord of the Church	Testimony of the Cross	Sword of the Spirit

Still, as accurately as my diagram provides a trinity of "centers," there is a single unity of focus: *Everything of our testimony is embodied in the Person of Jesus—the Person we worship!*

- He is the *Central Person*. The Father has categorically indicated that "it pleased [Him] that in [Christ] all the fullness should dwell" (Colossians 1:19), for "in [Christ] dwells all the fullness of the Godhead bodily" (Colossians 2:9). And regarding Jesus, the Father's words still resound from the Mount of Transfiguration: "Hear Him!" (Matthew 17:5; Mark 9:7; Luke 9:35).
- He is the *Center Point* of witness. Jesus has defined the Lord's table as His by merit of the fact that all that appears on it is solely to bear abiding testimony to His broken body and shed blood—the instruments that purchased and secured eternal salvation for all who will come to Him. "He who eats My flesh and drinks My blood abides in Me, and I in him" (John 6:56).
- He is the *Center Piece*. The Bible exists for one essential purpose: "These [Scriptures] are they which testify of Me" (John 5:39). For either by type, foreshadowing or direct mention, Messiah is the subject woven into the fabric of every book of the holy Scriptures. And in terms of its ultimate message, He is the Incarnate Word.

WHAT PLACE FOR CHRIST HIMSELF?

In every generation there are dynamics that press the Church to choose between ever-present points of either commitment or compromise. Stepping into the 21st century, we are no less confronted by this recurrent fact, and it is of maximum importance that the people of God discern where those present issues exist.

Some are more obvious than others. Spiritual leadership, for example, is being pressed on all sides either to confront or concede to moral and ethical drift, not only in society at large but even in the Church itself.

Such issues as the redefinition of marriage and the radical agenda related to required social acceptance of redefined sexual mores have called most biblically based believers to determine their positions and govern their lives and circles of influence accordingly.

Yet another issue is one about which the global Church is blurred—not lacking conviction so much as not understanding that the issue is as critically present as it is. The Church is confronted by the evolving working of the Holy Spirit with God's ancient people, the Jews, and especially as His sovereign purposes for them unfold in the political struggle over the state of Israel. Will the Church accede to the passivity that has caused Christians historically to yield to the forces of global anti-Semitism (e.g., the Holocaust)? Or will our collective voice and influence rise, informed by historical realities rather than brainwashed by a secularized press?

These matters, however significant each is in its own right, barely begin to note the spiritual and moral issues facing the Church.

And far above these, and beyond any other, is the issue to which every generation will be called to give account. Our generation, as each before it, must answer this question: What place is Christ Himself being given in His Church?

This question is not decided by councils, though they may affirm beliefs. It is not decided by doctrinal statements, though these may make biblically correct and soundly orthodox statements. Rather it is in the week-to-week lives of pastors and leaders and the worship life of the people who form local congregations that this question of "Who is Jesus and how will I [or we] relate to Him?" is decided. And it is that decision made in the worship place that will determine who Christ's people will be in their homes and the marketplace.

A WATERSHED ISSUE IN WORSHIP

We live in a day of a widely heralded and broadly welcomed renewal of worship. It is an awakening—a stirring across the nations, throughout the larger Body of Christ—and it is altering liturgies, creating new formats of approach to worship, transforming the musical atmosphere and opening up the Church's windows to fresh air and the sunlight of heaven in our midst.

Amid the renewal in form and style, however, the jury might well remain in consultation on this question: Is there a companion renewal—indeed, is there need for a revival— in the realm of understanding *about* worship? It does not require a critical eye, only an observant one, to answer this question. The answer is *YES!* The capital letters, italics and exclamation point are a studied and necessary emphasis.

Let me elaborate.

I am persuaded that we are at a point in the worship renewal that will, in the near future, result in either its proliferation with spiritual power or in its pollution through undiscerning confusion. The latter is already making waves, but the tide can still be turned to avoid the rise of mistaken ideas and habits traveling in the name of worship from inundating the lifestyle of many sectors of the Church that lack discernment.

Needed foremost is the reestablishment of a clear, unswerving focus on the Person we worship. Jesus, the Lord of the Church, the almighty Father, the Sovereign of the universe, the Holy Spirit, the Purifier as well as the power source of God's people—this is who we worship. But a watershed is at hand because it is seriously in doubt, even dubious, as to what degree the flow of worship is bathing souls in that understanding on a daily basis.

There are at least four reasons to raise this question.

1. The word *worship* itself has become so broadly defined as to be confused with music, rather than "prostrating oneself in spirit before the One to whom all worthiness should be ascribed."
2. Platform styles, while thankfully having moved from rigidly archaic to more communicatively contemporary, result too easily in the presenters becoming the focus of attention, rather than in worshipers being drawn to wonder, humility or a fresh yieldedness to the Lord.
3. The success of worship music in the marketplace has, with increasing subtlety, lured composers, artists and arrangers to succumb to a preoccupation with style rather than substance. While many exercise their gift with great sensitivity and spiritual stewardship, others—often younger and more vulnerable to temptation, as well as less discerning about where unwitting

deviation may compromise their mission—wander off course.

4 Solid lyrics set to music—the historic means by which the Church has obeyed the New Testament call to "let the word of Christ dwell in you richly" (Colossians 3:16)—too often become victim to a rampant preoccupation with "me," to a slothful attention to editing or to an impoverished grasp of God's Word.

In this regard David Bryant, in his book by the same title, laments a reduced evidence of "the supremacy of Christ" in the Church. This is a worthy concern, one I have noted in the decreasing appearance of pivotal concepts and decisive redemptive truths in the songs spreading today throughout the Church. The name of Jesus (or Christ), the blood of Christ (or the cross), the inclusion of passing or partial quotes of biblical phrases (the meaning of *psalms*), are among the concept casualties that need to be restored to this generation, to be fused into and laced through the minds, souls and heart of the worshiping Church.

I do not mean this observation as a blanket criticism of crisp creativity or youth-appealing or contemporary turns of phrase. I carry no brief for that style of criticism that every generation has faced in the aging naysayer who has nothing good to say about anything contemporary. I have spoken to more teens and college students in the last five years of my ministry than ever in my life. I serve pastorally in a congregation rich in talented contemporary artists and musicians who navigate the secular marketplace with skill and success. Most of the time I worship in a congregation that blends the most contemporary with the classically historic. Synthesizers and acoustic guitars will ignite praise as recent compositions of laud to God are received from around the world, while in the same service a three-manual organ will support the congregation's thundering forth with "And Can It Be That I Should Gain" or "Immortal, Invisible, God Only Wise." In short I am not a disgruntled theologian or nit-picking, carping critic of anything that stretches me beyond my comfort zone. I embrace worship music in all shapes and sizes.

Still I issue this trumpet sound, and it is not a solo piece. My acquaintance with such leaders as Don Moen, Darlene Zschech, Marcos Witt, Matt Redman, Marty Nystrom, Steve Green, Lamar Boschmann, Tommy Walker, Wayne and Libby Huirua and others confirms my concerns. While none of these is twenty-something or younger, their circle of involvement and many immediate associates suggest that they are not a company of the outdated or out of touch.

Further (and pardon my including myself!), together we constitute a group who, along with many other highly gifted musicians, artists and worship leaders, have carried the banner of worship into an era in which "contemporary" was at first rejected. Our concern now is that "contemporary" not become synonymous with either "confused," "carnally corrupted," "theologically barren" or "compromised in motive" to the point that the Person we worship pales in the shadows created by our preoccupation with stylized success, contemporary appeal or displacement of meaning with mere "music."

LET'S RAISE THE BAR—AND THE BANNER!

Two of the most effective uses of banners I have ever seen in a worship service took place in recent travels of mine.

Both were in well-ordered yet spiritually liberated Sunday morning gatherings at which I was speaking—one a Methodist church and one an Assembly of God. The striking thing to me was how effectively—at once tastefully and dynamically—the biblical concept of the waving or lifting of banners was applied: "We will rejoice in your salvation, and in the name of our God we will set up our banners!" (Psalm 20:5; see also Song of Solomon 6:4, 10).

What especially moved me was how the use of banners in both churches gloriously drew attention to Jesus Christ and moved the congregations to praise and magnify Him.

This stood in sharp contrast to several experiences I have had that were well-intended and doubtless sincere but either unwise or ungoverned, as souls moved randomly about the front of the sanctuary, flailing banners as they danced, sometimes artlessly and always distractingly. (I hasten to contrast this with many well-trained, disciplined and effectively choreographed worship dance teams I have seen who added as much to the worship as the other artists—singers and musicians—assisting the congregation to worthily exalt the Lord.)

In that Methodist church, glorious banners bearing the Savior's name were borne the length of the building as the congregation stood and the orchestra played "All Hail the Power of Jesus' Name." The people rose, less by any formal requirement than by the raw power of the moment that virtually drew you to your feet and caused your heart to join the anthem with high praise and upraised hands.

The turning point in Florida from a marvelous choral prelude, as worshipers gathered, to the beginning of the service, was with trumpet fanfare and the leader's summons of the people to their feet. The choir broke into song: "I want to see Jesus lifted high—a banner that flies across the land!" As they did, a cluster of banner-bearers began to file into the sanctuary, joyously waving the golden-hued silks as they led the congregation into a pronounced declaration of an unspoken yet obvious fact: Jesus Christ is Lord in this place!

My own heart resonated strongly—unsurprising since for all three decades of my pastoral leadership at The Church On The Way, there was hardly a Sunday that, at some point, the congregation did not rise to sing "All Hail the Power." This hymn was studied and crucial as part of our worship, usually sung near the beginning of the service, following a set of contemporary praise songs that opened the gathering. The people have never tired of it, just as they have never tired of our inclusion of a single, classic hymn each Sunday morning.

My strategic purposes in each of these practices: first, by means of singing "All Hail the Power," to lay down the Savior's calling card at the beginning of our service; and second, by means of the hymn, to teach in the way only a multi-versed, biblically substantive song can do. I also learned how dynamically the Holy Spirit can use older hymns to touch the chords of memory for people who experienced these songs in childhood. Many have testified to what this did for them—what Andre Crouch's song intones: "Take me back, take me back, dear Lord, to the place where I first believed You!"

A Word About "the Arts" and "Worship Concerts"

As contemporary communication becomes the open-door policy of more and more churches (and thankfully so), believers are faced with the challenge of balancing the

timely and the timeless. Whether we provide leadership in
the Church or are believers with a home or workplace
vocation, we are faced, with regard to the "new" in worship
music and church worship practices, with a need for
understanding, wisdom and discernment as to what is
Christ-centered and what is not.

Let me begin by asserting a prior conviction: In no way
do I believe that music, drama or artistry of any kind is
worthy only if it is "Christian." That is not only untrue but
hostile to the fundamental fact that God does remarkably
creative things through people, often even through ones
who do not know Him or honor His Son.

Yet.

I say *yet* because I believe that to dishonor God's worthy
creativity through a person, simply because he or she is yet
unconverted, is to slam a double door—the bottom half by
rejecting a person's gift here on earth, and the upper half
by refusing to honor the Giver-in-Heaven's grace through
that person.

I was in pastoral leadership nearly ten years before I got
"it"—the realization that with God there is no such thing
as a sacred/secular dichotomy. He has not divided the
world into the religious and the non-religious. Rather,
from heaven's perspective the division point is the dichotomy between light and darkness, between good and evil,
between the godly and the satanic, between the great
Creator God and the liar-deceiver Satan.

Consequently there is great reason to celebrate the rising
inclusion of the arts as well as music in more and more
evangelical churches and in their worship services. This is
potentially God-honoring in and of itself. But it is as
vulnerable to distortion and confusion as those things
we have observed that so easily distract from the real

mission of the Church. This is another matter that calls us to increase our discernment; to refuse to become so enchanted by our expanding acknowledgment of *creativity* that we neglect to keep our focus fixed on the *Creator*. Romans 1:21–25 reveals the inevitably perverse that will intrude wherever humans end in glorifying the creature or the creative more than the Creator; and there is no wall of division that preempts the same happening with believers.

Worship and worship services need to keep their focus clear. Serving in a congregation filled with incredibly gifted artists, and wanting to see their gifts released to inspire and encourage others, I know firsthand the challenge of maintaining discernment in this area. For my part, the key has been distinguishing between worship and edification. The former is a presentation to God; the latter is a presentation to man. We need to distinguish between the two in our understanding, in our open welcome of the artistic and in our public deployment of the arts or our private enjoyment of the same.

Much that is done when artistry is platformed in Church (or enjoyed by a believer) does bring insight, inspiration and edifying content to us. And I agree that such a presentation or performance by an artist may, for that individual, be an act of worship to God as he or she presents the gift in ministry unto His glory. The message of "The Little Drummer Boy" illustrates this concept, and there is no reason to doubt that God is well pleased with such gifts. It is also inescapable, however, that for many who witness an artist, worshiping God is not really their response. Amazement, appreciation, exclamatory acknowledgment, even with applause that includes God in the tribute, is not the equivalent of worshiping the Lord.

In What Way Are People Moved?

This brings me to a delicate point of distinguishing between
an accepted practice in contemporary musical arrangement
and what I see as not generally acceptable in a worship
service. It is a practice that stems from the marvelous
evolution of "worship concerts" as a means of evangelism—a practice that is (thankfully) spreading globally, as
God is praised in gatherings in which the attractive nature
of the contemporary music and artists draws people into
an exposure to the testimony of the Gospel. Whether
choirs, bands, groups or individual artists, I applaud it all,
especially when the performers are people who "have their
heads on straight with Jesus" and who are living lives
consistent with those who are disciples of His.

In noting the worth of these settings, we have an
immediate illustration of the difference between worship
and edification, because most of what takes place in the
average worship concert is not, at least at the beginning,
something that moves *people* (draws them to God) as much
as it simply *moves* people (more specifically, draws them to
the music). This is no argument against the strategy of
starting with the music as a strategic means to evangelize,
but it is a point of discernment because of a growing habit I
observe in the Church at large.

Musical arrangements designed for concert presentation
are increasingly the same ones used in worship services.
While that appropriation may work in many cases, the
"concert" tradition of extended instrumental interludes
within a piece—e.g., giving eight bars to the drummer, the
guitarist and a wind instrument to "get in their licks,"
much to the delight of the audience and manifest in its
applause for each artist—is not, to my view, consistent with

a worship service. The issue is not that this is sinful; it is simply not productive to the intention of a worship service.

In short, you cannot import a concert style into a real worship gathering. They are two different things, neither of which ought to be confused with the other.

THE ULTIMACY OF CHRIST

Early in my ministry I was touched by a book written by Robert Speer, a Presbyterian missionary who left a marvelous witness in his work, *The Finality of Jesus Christ*. That theme might well have been the title to the epistle to the Hebrews, which is where I would like to conclude this chapter.

Perhaps no book in the whole of God's Word summarizes so succinctly and penetratingly how appropriate it is that Jesus Himself—His worship, His praise and His glorious honoring—becomes the focus and essence of everything we think about, plan, prepare for, arrange, produce, program and *do* when we worship. His honor and glory must be the ultimate objective of all we pursue as worshipers, whether we lead or follow. His ultimacy is revealed clearly in the Word of God: All worship must flow from that fountain of revelation so as to maintain a full and worthily glorifying perspective on Him.

As the Holy Spirit takes us into the Word and unto the Savior—and then by means of our worship services brings us together to magnify His name, that others may be drawn to Him as we lift Him up—worship's glorious purpose may be realized. That is why I urge all who would worship, and even more so all who would lead, to keep filled with the Word. From that source the Holy Spirit will readily over-flow our spirits with Christ, renew our minds through the truth, influence our thoughts with His love and control our lives by His Kingdom rule and presence—all preparing and fully animating our worship

Let's allow all that characterizes the entire book of Hebrews to shape the character of our worship. Its pages elaborate the supremacy, finality and ultimacy of our wonderful Savior. The epistle's opening words announce, *Jesus is the Message*: "God, who at various times and in various ways spoke in time past to the fathers by the prophets, has in these last days spoken to us by His Son..." (Hebrews 1:1–2).

The opening three verses of Hebrews 1 make seven statements about our Lord Jesus Christ. Each should be explored as they might be elsewhere in the Scriptures, for an inexhaustible mine of truth waits to be found in each statement. It is impossible to spend time with passages like this and not be conditioned to keep our perspective when we worship!

The Person we worship is:

- the predestined Heir of all things (verse 2);
- the avenue of God's power by whom the world was made (verse 2);
- the radiant Representative of God's glory shown to humankind (verse 3);
- the ultimate expression of the ultimate reality (verse 3);
- the Sustainer of all that exists in the universe (verse 3);
- the Savior from sin and Redeemer of sinful humankind (verse 3); and
- the exalted and ascended Lord—His Majesty on high (verse 3).

This is the One to whom we come with our praise and thanksgiving. He is the One whose love and grace prompt our rejoicing and laudation. His Father, our Creator, is the exceedingly glorious One who gave us this Jesus. His commissioned Comforter, the Holy Spirit, is the One sent to us to overflow us with enabling power and give us the capacity to glorify Him—Jesus, our Lord.

> Sing that name to me, in sweetest harmony,
> Whisper tenderly the name of Jesus,
>> Jesus,
>>> Jesus.
> Sing that name, praise the name of
> Jesus Christ the Lord.
> Captives are set free, souls at liberty,
> Darkness made to flee when you sing Jesus,
>> Jesus,
>>> Jesus.
> Sing that name, praise the name of
> Jesus Christ the Lord.

Let anthems be raised as hearts, hands and voices do the same. The wisest and strongest thing we can do to lead people in worship is to teach them about Jesus. As they grow in knowing more of *who* He is, genuine worship will ceaselessly arise, worshiping hearts will be healed and transformed, and shock waves of spiritual vitality will shatter the darkness in our part of the world.

PART 2

THE POWER OF WORSHIP

We Lift Our Voice Rejoicing

We lift our voice rejoicing because the Lord above
Has sent His Son to save us, and manifest His love.
Let ev'ry hill re-echo with this the song we raise,
"To Him whose Blood has bought us be glory, pow'r and
      praise."

We lift our eyes in faith to the Cross whereon He died.
Redeemed at matchless price, now in Christ we're justified.
His Blood has washed our garments, His peace has filled our
      souls.
The Cross is now our glory since grace has made us whole.

We lift our hearts to worship the conquering Savior's name.
Our tongues speak forth the praises of Him Who is the same.
Christ Jesus reigns in power throughout eternity.
As yesterday, so now, and forever He shall be.

[Refrain]
We praise You, O Father, unspeakable our joy.
In Christ our hearts find glory sin's pow'r cannot destroy.

J. W. H.

CHAPTER 7

The Beauty of Holiness

The Purifying Power of Worship

"For Yours is the kingdom and the power and the glory forever. Amen."

Matthew 6:13

Worship is the fountainhead of all power. The release of God's purpose in our lives and the restoration of His rulership on earth happen through the power of worship. When the resurrected Jesus drew His disciples together at Galilee, it was following their worship of Him that the Lord gave the Great Commission. Indeed the Church was *commissioned* in a worship service:

> Then the eleven disciples went away into Galilee, to the mountain which Jesus had appointed for them. When they saw Him, they worshiped Him; but some doubted. And Jesus came and spoke to them, saying, "All authority has been

given to Me in heaven and on earth. Go therefore and make
disciples of all the nations, baptizing them in the name of
the Father and of the Son and of the Holy Spirit, teaching
them to observe all things that I have commanded you; and
lo, I am with you always, even to the end of the age." Amen.

Matthew 28:16–20

The Church was also *born* in a worship service. At
Pentecost it was the worship of the Lord at a miraculous
dimension, not the proclamation of the Gospel, that
attracted the people and ushered in the power of God's
Kingdom (see Acts 2:1–13). It is here that we see fulfillment
of the promise of power given earlier by the Lord:

"You shall receive power when the Holy Spirit has come
upon you; and you shall be witnesses to Me in Jerusalem,
and in all Judea and Samaria, and to the end of the earth."

Acts 1:8

Yet at both the Galilean encounter and at Pentecost,
people resisted. Even among those who were closest to
Jesus, "some doubted" (Matthew 28:17). And at Pentecost
the exuberant worship offended the tastes of some who
mocked the worshipers as "full of new wine" (Acts 2:13).

The same thing happens today. Even when, as at Pentecost, there is an effusion of the Spirit, with the purpose of
God being fulfilled, there are still those who doubt, mock or
get offended.

Doubt is not necessarily a disqualification for being His
chosen servant. But it is a hindrance to our faith and our
worship. Since the disciples were present among the 120
through whom the Holy Spirit flowed with power at
Pentecost, it seems safe to assume that all the disciples
overcame their doubt. The power of worship has a way of
crowding out doubt and releasing vital faith.

Throughout Scripture, wherever the Church is at prayer or in worship, there is a great release of power. Probably the most notable case is recorded in Acts 13 where, following a time of worship, when the believers "ministered to the Lord and fasted" (verse 2), the Holy Spirit instructed them to release Paul and Barnabas for the work to which He was calling them. And what took place by the direction of the Holy Spirit in a worship meeting at Antioch twenty centuries ago shaped the very flow of history and the course of Western civilization.

WORSHIP CONFRONTS CARNAL PRIDE

True biblical worship requires openness, forthrightness, acknowledgment of need and presentation of self. Worship confronts the fear and pride inherent in human flesh. We are all beset by the carnality that causes us to fear what other people may think of us; it can dominate me as a pastor when I am hesitant to lead in the manner God is directing because I am afraid of offending some. Yet when we commit ourselves to serve Him in the way God intends, we experience the release of His divine power and purpose in our lives.

A pivotal moment in my own ministry and the life of our church occurred shortly after I took the pastorate of The Church On The Way. It was in October 1970 during the worship portion of our service, with about sixty people present, that a woman brought forth a word of prophecy. I happened to be seated at the organ, being the only person there who could play it. The young man leading the service had not really known how to deal with the prophecy, and I remember feeling disturbed that the congregation had not responded to it. I slipped off the organ bench and walked to the front of the church to speak to the congregation, aware of the fact that a family of five was visiting and seated at the back.

When you have only sixty or so people in the congregation, five visitors is a sizable addition! Hoping they might decide to join the church, I did not want to offend them in any way. So as I crossed to the front of the church, I remember having to make a decision. Would I concern myself with the reasonable comfort of those five people or be obedient to what I knew God was saying?

Expressing my desire to the guests not to embarrass them in any way, I challenged the congregation about how we were going to respond to the word of prophecy. I told them I believed we needed to make up our minds right then that when God spoke to us as a church, we would do what He said and not concern ourselves with what people thought. I was making up my own mind, I announced, that from that day on I would always lead this congregation in worship. I would do it as graciously and tastefully as possible; nevertheless I would seek to be guided only by what God desired. The congregation gave their clear assent to what I had said, after which we sang, and a beautiful spirit of praise began to rise.

That day we turned a monumental corner. A demonic spirit that had been oppressing the church was broken, and a glorious liberty began to attend our worship. Two months later the Lord manifested His glory in our sanctuary.

The power of worship is locked up in this truth: When people commit themselves to worship, the Lord will dwell among them in power. And as they abide in worship, He will not only dwell in their midst, but develop His life and extend Jesus' Kingdom rule among them.

Worship releases the purpose, power and pathway of what God wants to do in His Church; and it establishes the climate in which people begin to learn a true submission to God, to one another and to church leadership.

WORSHIP CREATES A PLACE TO REINSTATE GOD'S RULE

What took place at the Fall of man caused the loss of our relationship with our heavenly Father and our ordained rulership of this planet. By Adam's sin humankind was separated from fellowship with God, and it ceded to the prince of darkness the partnership and dominion of earth that He intended for us.

Worship is essential to God's plan of redemption and provides a strategic avenue for His entry into an alienated world. It is the means by which God generates the power for His rule to be extended—for evangelism, sacrificial giving, intercession and breaking up the strongholds of hell. Where worship is released, God's presence comes to dwell, and where God's presence abides, there will be power. As a result the works of darkness are frustrated and the operations of hell begin to be counterattacked by people with whom God has restored fellowship and in whose midst He is able to reveal Himself by His presence and power.

Human worship is *man beginning;* holiness of worship is *man becoming.* Through our worship we are transformed from His sons and daughters into His kings and priests (see Revelation 1:6). We become ministering agents of His Kingdom assigned to extend that Kingdom on earth.

Nowhere is this truth made clearer than in the keys to effective prayer that Jesus gave His disciples in Matthew 6.

Without keys things do not work. You can sit in your car as long as you want and complain that it is not moving, but you cannot drive unless you use the key. The Lord says He has given to us "the keys of the kingdom" (Matthew 16:19).

Jesus taught us to pray first by using the key of our restored *access* through relationship to God—"Our Father in heaven"—followed by our worship of Him: "Hallowed be Your name" (Matthew 6:9). Then His prayer extends the invitation of His presence and dominion: "Your kingdom come. Your will be done on earth as it is in heaven" (verse 10). When we pray in the manner that Jesus taught His disciples, we are first, with worship, reaching into the invisible realm, and then, on the grounds of that worship, welcoming the entry of His divine authority, rulership and power into this world.

THE RESTORATIVE POWER OF WORSHIP

Many precious people will go to heaven completely loved by God, without having learned to exercise the power of worship. God's saving grace is not released according to our worship; that was accomplished at Calvary. His power and glory, however, *are* released in proportion to our worship, capacitating us for the establishing of His Kingdom on earth.

While our sins are atoned for at the cross, human beings become truly restored in ourselves only when we worship God and when, brought into fellowship with others, we confront our fear and pride. Then, through our worship, we find the release of divine power and purpose in our lives. The power of our worship not only opens the way for the restoration of Kingdom rule on earth; it also restores the King's wholeness to our lives, as illustrated in Isaiah 6:1–8.

During a time of national crisis following the death of Uzziah, king of Judah, Isaiah was seeking the Lord. In a vision he was transported into the presence of God and saw the *shekinah* glory (here described as "smoke") and the angelic beings that surround the throne of God:

> In the year that King Uzziah died, I saw the Lord sitting on a throne, high and lifted up, and the train of His robe filled the temple. Above it stood seraphim; each one had six wings: with two he covered his face, with two he covered his feet, and with two he flew. And one cried to another and said:
>
> "Holy, holy, holy is the LORD of hosts;
> The whole earth is full of His glory!"
>
> And the posts of the door were shaken by the voice of him who cried out, and the house was filled with smoke.
>
> Isaiah 6:1–4

Although Isaiah loved the Lord and was a man we would call godly, his response to the ineffable holiness and glory of God's throne brought him to a horrible sense of his own unworthiness and failure:

> So I said:
>
> "Woe is me, for I am undone!
> Because I am a man of unclean lips,
> And I dwell in the midst of a people of unclean lips;
> For my eyes have seen the King,
> The LORD of hosts."
>
> verse 5

The Greek word for "worthy" was *axios*, which originally described a coin of valuable metals that was worth its full weight, just as years ago in America, a twenty-dollar gold piece would have contained twenty dollars' worth of gold. In the ancient world, when minting processes were in their early development, coins would wear thin and lose some of their actual value. They would weigh less and thus become worth less. To us the word *worthless* implies worth nothing, but it actually means worth *less*.

This is exactly what Isaiah is saying he feels about himself. We have already looked at the longing every human being has for the *weight* of God's glory—His *chabod*—in our lives. Isaiah senses that his life has lost some of its value. He wants to do the right thing but, faced with the awesome holiness of God, he feels unworthy.

We often feel "undone" just as Isaiah felt. We do not seem to be able to pull our lives together; we feel unworthy and unholy. Just as, after years of use and handling, the face can be worn off a coin, so there come times when the image of the Living God on our lives and the wholeness of our character seem to have worn thin. We may have lost our sensitivity to God's will; we may feel we have become just so much "small change." In the face of this, our loving Father God calls us to enter His presence in order that a transfer of His being and nature into ours can take place. God desires to remint and restore the worth of our lives by pouring His worth into us.

Through worship, the worth that has been worn off our lives can be restored.

THE PURIFYING FIRE OF WORSHIP

Our awareness of our sin and failure before the Lord happens not that we might be condemned, but that we might be restored. Even Isaiah, who loved and served God faithfully, was overwhelmed when confronted by a vision of God's glory. In one way or another we all feel what Isaiah felt. Later on Isaiah goes so far as to describe our righteousness as "filthy rags" (64:6). That truth breeds a natural hesitation to approach the Lord and worship. Yet God's heart is so gracious toward us that, just as He did with Isaiah, He desires to meet you and me at the point of our need so He can purify and restore us.

In the vision Isaiah was describing, an angel commissioned by the Lord came to him:

> Then one of the seraphim flew to me, having in his hand a live coal which he had taken with the tongs from the altar. And he touched my mouth with it, and said:
>
> > "Behold, this has touched your lips;
> > Your iniquity is taken away,
> > And your sin purged."
>
> Isaiah 6:6–7

With the holy fire of God, the angel touched the part of Isaiah's body that he felt impure about, his lips, not to burn him up but to purge and restore him. I am persuaded that if Isaiah had said, "I am a man of unclean hands," the angel would have taken the coal and touched his hands. If he had said, "I am a man of unclean mind," the angel would have touched his mind. The fire of the coal brought regeneration to the place of impurity that Isaiah was most sensitive to.

As such the fire of worship gives us a picture of how God's restoration works in our lives:

- It *refines* us—burning out the residue of what is unworthy.
- It *consumes* us—taking the bondage out of our lives and burning it up.

- It *melts* and *warms* us—softening hard hearts and thawing out cold ones.
- It *ignites* us when we have turned off, God turns us back on.

At whatever is the point of our greatest weakness, the Lord invites us to come to Him in worship where, in the midst of His holiness, we can be touched and restored by His holy, purifying fire.

HOLINESS IS WHOLENESS, ACTIVATED BY WORSHIP

In Isaiah's vision the angelic beings gathered around the throne are worshiping God with these words: "Holy, holy, holy is the LORD of hosts; the whole earth is full of His glory!" (verse 3).

Every time we are given a glimpse into the throne room of God, we always see worship and hear the words *Holy, holy, holy* being spoken. The focus is on God's holiness. There is a root relationship between the words *whole, health, wholeness* and *holy. Holiness* is being whole at the spiritual level. When I am born again, I am called a holy person, a saint: I am made whole before God. Essentially holiness is God's entirety entering my incompleteness. The way that happens is when we come into His presence with worship. Psalm 16:11 says that in His presence we will find "fullness of joy." We come to the One who is holy in order that our inadequacies and failures may be purged and replaced with His wholeness.

God calls His people to worship Him and to "be holy": "As He who called you is holy, you also be holy in all your conduct, because it is written, 'Be holy, for I am holy'" (1 Peter 1:15–16; also see Leviticus 11:45; Matthew 5:48).

For many years I saw holiness as a requirement and, like most people, was terrified. God seemed to be saying, "You must do this because I do it." But I have come to see that this is not Father God's heart in these words at all. Just as we inherit certain characteristics from our biological parents so, as we worship, the image and nature of our heavenly Father begin to be manifested in our lives.

From my father and my grandfather, I inherited the genetics for a balding head and a larger-than-usual nose. But my daddy never once came to me and said, "Son, about the time you're 25 I want you to start losing hair." Nor did he tell me, "Before you go to sleep, strain really hard and try to get your nose to grow a bit bigger." I just came to look this way because my father's nature is in me.

In the same way my heavenly Father says, "My life and likeness are in you; you will be holy because I am holy." I came to realize that His call to "be holy, for I am holy" is not a requirement; it is a *promise*.

The fact that God is holy relates not to our shame and condemnation but to our healing and restoration. As we worship, His image and nature begin to become manifest in our lives. We *will* be holy because our Father is holy. That is a promise.

COMMISSIONED BY THE POWER OF GOD TO "GO . . ."

It was in the place of worship, after Isaiah was purified and restored, that God gave him a mission: "Also I heard the voice of the LORD, saying: 'Whom shall I send, and who will go for Us?' Then I said, 'Here am I! Send me.' And He said, 'Go...'" (Isaiah 6:8–9).

Once again a redeemed, restored servant of the Lord is commissioned by the power of God to "Go...." The mission and purpose of our lives, our destiny as Jesus' disciples, is found in the context of worship and His power to accomplish all that He intends of restoration and ruler-ship in us.

CHAPTER 8

A Place for the King

The Biblical Foundation for Worship

> Coming to Him as to a living stone, rejected indeed by men, but chosen by God and precious, you also, as living stones, are being built up a spiritual house, a holy priesthood, to offer up spiritual sacrifices acceptable to God through Jesus Christ.
>
> 1 Peter 2:4–5

The living God dwells where His people worship, and *life* happens where He dwells. It is my conviction, therefore, that the life-flow of a church congregation will rise only as high as their worship of the Godhead. We cannot underestimate the importance of teaching the Word of God, but the Word itself reveals that worship is what the Church is all about.

The book of Ephesians says that we who trust in Christ are to be "to the praise of His glory" (1:12), "built together for a dwelling place of God in the Spirit" (2:22). Peter describes the people of God as "living stones . . . being built up a spiritual house, a holy priesthood" (1 Peter 2:5). Each member of the Body is a part of the temple of the Lord, summoned to be a "living stone" of His dwelling.

God is looking for a place to dwell. We know of nowhere else in the universe except earth where God is not praised or welcomed. In the words of Jesus Himself, "Foxes have holes and birds of the air have nests, but the Son of Man has nowhere to lay His head" (Matthew 8:20). During His ministry, Jesus had no home. When He was born, there was no room at the inn (see Luke 2:7). In one sense, this is just an interesting analogy, but in another, it is a dramatic demonstration of the fact that God has a hard time finding a place to be on this planet.

In order for the foundation of our "spiritual house" to be firmly established, it is important that we understand the biblical grounds for worship. These derive from the saga of loss and recovery of humankind's fellowship with the almighty God.

STAGE 1: LOST AUTHORITY

Humanity is given dominion of the planet and gives it away.

In Genesis 1:26, we see humankind given rule and dominion over the earth: "Then God said, 'Let Us make man in Our image, according to Our likeness; let them have dominion . . . over all the earth and over every creeping thing that creeps on the earth.'"

Authority over this planet and all its creatures was delegated to Adam from the Creator. Adam was given everything and was asked to obey God in only one thing. In violating that one thing, not only did Adam lose his relationship with God, but also the dominion he had been given was lost (see Genesis 3).

Had that been all, it would have been bad enough. Man now lives on the planet without the right to rule over it, his relationship with the Creator has been severed and he must earn his living by the sweat of his brow. Loss of dominion also means that we now have an animal kingdom in turmoil.

And there is more. The consequences of Adam's disobedience are far greater. When Adam violated the trust God gave him by obeying the suggestions of another being, Adam *submitted himself to another power.* By so doing, he transferred the title deed to this planet into the hands of the serpent—Satan—whom Jesus referred to as "the prince of this world" (John 12:31, KJV). When Satan showed Jesus "all the kingdoms of the world and their glory" and propositioned Him, "All these things I will give You if You will fall down and worship me" (Matthew 4:8–9), Jesus denied the terms, but He did not challenge Satan's right to make the offer.

The Kingdom of God, intended to be administrated by man on earth, has been crowded off the planet by the kingdom of darkness. God could have taken back rulership, of course, but His desire has always been that the human race He created should rule the planet. Dominion was lost because of man's *choice.* God, out of His unfathomable nature of love, gave humankind the freedom to make that choice, just as He now graciously invites human beings to choose to receive eternal life through His Son, Jesus. Out of

His perfect love, God did not—and does not—impose His rule.

Nevertheless, not everything has been lost by the fall of humanity into sin. Human beings are still created in the image of God. And we still have the right and the capacity to make our own choices. God desires for human beings to choose Him as their King, so that His Kingdom rule and blessings may be manifest on earth through them (see Matthew 6:9–10).

STAGE 2: MINISTRY FROM WITHIN

The Lord begins the plan of redemption—the Levitical priesthood.

In the Old Testament, God prepares to introduce His King, setting the stage for the redemption of earth. He begins with Abraham, through whose offspring He intends to recover the planet and bless all its nations (see Genesis 17). But His chosen people—the children of Israel—wind up enslaved in Egypt. He then summons Moses, using him to deliver Israel, and declares His desire to make Israel "a kingdom of priests and a holy nation" (Exodus 19:6).

God's original intent was that *all* Israel would be "priests." This plan was short-circuited, however, when the people rebelled against Moses' leadership following the fashioning of the golden calf. Only the Levites stood by Moses. As a result of this key incident, priesthood in the nation of Israel became restricted to this one tribe (see Exodus 32). (By the way, we should not give the Levites too much credit for their loyalty on this occasion, since they were prompted mostly by tribal affiliation to Moses.)

In the New Testament, we learn that Jesus desires for *all* those who name Him their Lord to be His ministering "priests." In an interesting parallel of the Old Testament experience, Church tradition singles out the "priesthood" as a select few. So instead of all the people of God reaching out to minister to the world, we end up with a segment of the Church ministering to itself—just as the priests of Israel ministered only to Israel.

Yet look at what the Scriptures say about the Church serving as ministering agents of Jesus Christ: "To Him who loved us and washed us from our sins in His own blood, and *has made us kings and priests* to His God and Father, to Him be glory and dominion forever and ever. Amen" (Revelation 1:5–6, emphasis added).

Some people take these verses to mean that we will reign on earth when Jesus returns. But John is speaking in the *past tense*: The text says that "He *loved* us and *washed* us"— and we know this has already happened. Then John says, "He *has made* us kings and priests"—again, the tense of the verb indicates that this has already happened. We are His kings (who have dominion) and His priests (who worship) *now*. (This is not to discount the millennial rule; simply speaking, we do not have to rule *all* the earth to rule some of it.)

STAGE 3: THE LESSONS BEGIN

The Lord introduces the role of worship.

When the Lord God appeared to Moses in the burning bush, He told him, "When you have brought the people out of Egypt, you shall *serve God* on this mountain" (Exodus

3:12, emphasis added). The Hebrew word that is used here for "serve"—*abad*—also means to be a servant of, or to worship. By saying they would "serve God," He meant that His people would worship Him. It took only one day for God to deliver the Ten Commandments, but His people remained at Mount Sinai for more than a year, building the Tabernacle and being taught by God how to worship. As we have seen, God's plan for redemption, recovery of fellowship and resumed dominion was that His people would be priests, and *priests lead worship.*

Human beings would never be able to take back this planet in their own strength. Only in the context of their relationship with Him and the dominion that flows from His throne was the power of God ever going to touch earth. Hence, His deep desire to teach them about worship.

STAGE 4: THE BOUNDARIES GROW

Worship is expanded under David's monarchy.

David's reign saw both the boundaries of worship and the boundaries of territorial land expand in an unprecedented manner. David had a heart for worship and taught his people a great deal about praising the Lord out loud. He wrote many of the psalms, which ultimately became the early Church's handbook for worship. Under David's leadership, the use of instruments and choirs was expanded. These things were not new in the worship of Israel, but they began to be systematized and structured in a way that reveals the important place worship occupied in the nation's life.

David also built a second Tabernacle. No one knows what happened to the first one; it may have fallen into disrepair during the reign of Saul. Passionate to see God's presence established in the midst of the people, David made a place for the Tabernacle in the heart of the nation. Although it was his desire to build a Temple, the Lord fulfilled that through his son Solomon—and, just as He had done with the Tabernacle, God filled the Temple with His glory (see 1 Kings 8). Tragically, however, because of the sins of the people, the Temple of Solomon was destroyed. And with that loss, Israel entered the years of exile.

It is important to underscore that under David's leadership, there was a correlation between the expansion of Israel's territorial boundaries and the expansion of the boundaries of its worship. As their worship grew, so did their dominion. The same holds true for the Church today: It expands in dominion in direct proportion to its worship. Indeed, I firmly believe that worship is the key to evangelism.

STAGE 5: VICTORY OVER DARKNESS

God's own Son comes and "tabernacles" among us.

Jesus Christ epitomizes and personifies both the *Tabernacle* and the *Temple* where the glory of God dwells: "And the Word became flesh and dwelt among us, and we beheld His glory, the glory as of the only begotten of the Father, full of grace and truth" (John 1:14).

The word translated here as "dwelt" is the Greek word *skenoo*, which could equally be translated "tabernacled."

Similarly, Jesus refers to Himself as the temple in John 2:19: "Destroy this temple, and in three days I will raise it up."

Everywhere Jesus goes, He proclaims that the Kingdom of God is present because He, the King, is there. For the first time since Adam, there is a sinless man on the planet, and Jesus overcomes where Adam failed. He is here to establish a new breed of human beings—"a chosen generation, a royal priesthood, a holy nation, His own special people, that you may proclaim the praises of Him who called you out of darkness into His marvelous light" (1 Peter 2:9). These are the people whom God will use to reclaim the planet, and the way they will do that is *through their worship*.

For the same reason as the Temple of Solomon was destroyed, so Jesus—the living Temple of God's glory—is destroyed on the cross: because of the sins of the people. Yet the Bible tells us that if Satan had had any inkling of God's plan, he never would have wanted to see the crucifixion take place:

> But we speak the wisdom of God in a mystery, the hidden wisdom which God ordained before the ages for our glory, which none of the rulers of this age knew; for had they known, they would not have crucified the Lord of glory.
>
> 1 Corinthians 2:7–8

There, at the cross, where Satan thought he had once again succeeded in expanding his "principalities and powers," the Bible says he was disarmed by Jesus who triumphed over them, making his kingdom of darkness into a "public spectacle" (see Colossians 2:15).

Not only does Jesus win victory over death on the cross, but by the power of His resurrection, He becomes the seed that, having fallen into the ground and died, then begins to bear fruit. All over the planet, He begets people who receive the power of His life and begin to come alive with dominion possibility, bringing the rule, power and presence of God to all the earth. No longer does man have to labor in the power of his flesh; now, the power of the Kingdom of God is "at hand" (Mark 1:15).

STAGE 6: A GODLY HABITATION

Jesus prepares the Church to be a temple of living stones.

The Lord is now ready to build His people into a dwelling place for His presence. Jesus has prepared the Church to be a temple built of "living stones"—that's you and me! When we gather together, we become a place for God to dwell and for the dominion of His Kingdom to be established; the King is literally "enthroned" in our praises (Psalm 22:3). When we worship, God will come and dwell with us, with all the weight of His glory, His rulership and His dominion.

In this atmosphere—where worship ushers in the presence of God—four critically important things take place. First, the Word becomes *incarnated* in people; it becomes life, not just an intellectual exercise. Second, people are *healed* in the ongoing pattern of God's presence. Third, they come to *know the Lord* as His Kingdom is established. And, finally, as God *empowers* His people, their worship *crowds out* the borders of hell's domain.

When we come together in a worship service, God's people are built up as a habitation for His presence, as the "living stones" of His temple. Through our worship, an intimate and vibrant relationship with the living God is made possible: His assignment for us as His "royal priest-hood" is restored; we become ministering agents of His resurrection life to the world; and we are enabled to move in the expanding dominion and rulership He intended for humankind from the beginning.

CHAPTER 9

Worship That Possesses the Land

The Promise of Worship

> Then the LORD appeared to Abram and said, "To your descendants I will give this land." And there he built an altar to the LORD, who had appeared to him.
>
> Genesis 12:7

God gave Abraham[1] a promise of greatness and significance, that He was going to do something with Abraham's life that would bring him to an appointed destiny:

> "Get out of your country...
> To a land that I will show you....
> I will bless you
> And make your name great;
> And you shall be a blessing.

I will bless those who bless you,
And I will curse him who curses you;
And in you all the families of the earth shall be blessed."

Genesis 12:1–3

It is not surprising that God makes the same promise of significance and destiny to you and me because in Romans 4, the Bible says that we who are in Christ are the spiritual offspring of Abraham, who is often referred to as the "father of faith."

As He did with Abraham, the Lord calls us out to come and follow Him; He promises to transform our lives progressively into the likeness and image of Himself that He intended us to be; He desires to increase and overflow us with His blessings that we may become a light in the darkness to others; and He seeks our devotion and commitment to enter into fellowship with Him in order to fulfill His plan of redemption for our world.

He accomplishes all of this by first *meeting us where we worship.*

Abraham's building of altars preceded the building of the Tabernacle, yet even after the Tabernacle's completion at Sinai, altars were an important part of Israel's worship—in fact, worshipers encountered an altar of brass before they could even approach the Tabernacle.

The Bible says that Abraham was a man who made his moves on the basis of personal encounters with God, and that he erected an altar at each site of those encounters as a monument to something the Lord spoke into or was doing in His life. For Abraham, the building of altars firmed up God's promise to him; they became milestones in his life and walk with God—testaments to worship-filled encounters with the power and presence of the Most Holy Lord.

THE BLUEPRINT FOR BUILDING ALTARS

God's presence is welcomed where His people worship, attending in proportional response to our passionate hunger and thirst for Him (see Matthew 5:6). Whenever people gather together to worship Jesus Christ corporately "in spirit and truth," a vital sense of expectancy, faith and ministry takes place. Hope rises, joy abounds, tears of gratitude and repentance flow, hearts are touched and melted in humility. His graciousness and love is poured out.

But the dynamic experienced by people in church does not happen because of the personality or quick-wittedness of leadership—it does not come because of the beautiful stained glass windows, the glossy wooden pews or even by the accomplished technique of the musicians or the choir.

The dynamic we encounter is a manifestation of the glory of the Lord responding to our heartfelt, passionate worship of Him. It is our worship that welcomes the presence of the Lord, and the same thing that can happen in a church service can happen in our homes, in the places where *we* dwell. Like Abraham, we can build a place of intimate personal encounter with the Lord wherever we are. You and I can build a house of worship where we live.

In fact, the Lord promises in His Word that one day, His glory will rest above "every dwelling place" in Mount Zion —the heavenly Jerusalem of Revelation, just as was true over the Tabernacle of Israel. The prophet Isaiah writes:

> Then the LORD will create above every dwelling place of Mount Zion, and above her assemblies, a cloud and smoke by day and the shining of a flaming fire by night. For over

all the glory there will be a covering. And there will be a tabernacle for shade in the daytime from the heat, for a place of refuge, and for a shelter from storm and rain.

Isaiah 4:5–6

The day will come when what happened over the corporate worship of Israel will happen over *every home* of the redeemed—people will receive the evidence of God's glory in the blessing of His shelter (the cloud by day), as well as the security of His protection (the pillar of fire by night). In that setting, God will set His glory upon every dwelling, making it a place of refuge and defense.

In looking at the example set by our "father of faith" Abraham, we can discern our own "blueprint" for building altars of worship that welcome the promises and presence of God in our lives.

Build an Altar Wherever You Are

In response to the voice of the Lord, Abraham journeyed to the land of the Canaanites, unquestionably one of the most vicious and corrupt cultures in history. Canaanite worship involved child sacrifice and cult prostitution, and in time, the Lord would hand their land over to the Israelites and commission them to annihilate its people.

It is here amidst a society of grotesque wickedness and immoral worship that God told Abraham, "To your descendants I will give this land" (Genesis 12:7). Abraham's "promised land" was ruled by a pagan culture devoted to carnality and Satan worship. We can just imagine the thoughts that might go through our own minds if we found ourselves in this situation: *You call this a place where I'm supposed to raise a family and get blessed?* Yet Abraham was a man of *faith*—though he was standing in the middle of everything that seemed to be the exact opposite of a promise, he acknowledged the Lord and built an altar.

God intends that something in us be both "altared" (that is, *humbled* before Him) as well as "altered" (that is, *transformed*) when we encounter Him in worship. We have all at one time or another sensed anticipation of a promise that God has put in our hearts and that we find underwritten in His Word. Yet often the way that promise becomes fulfilled may be much different than the way we thought it would be.

Trusting that God was able to transform the situation, Abraham chose to embrace His promise and to make the place where he had been sent a place of worship to the Lord instead of second-guessing Him and deciding that it would be better to move on. Rather than try to change a difficult situation on his own, Abraham *worshiped* and *welcomed* the Almighty into it.

Surely there are things that each of us would like to see changed—in ourselves, in our families, in our workplaces or in the society in which we live. In today's world, corruption is virtually on the altar of the business and entertainment industries. Immoral lifestyles are taught as acceptable in our schools. The enemy seeks to drain off every reference to God from America's national life. In the midst of things that grate our souls and threaten our peace, the Lord says, in effect, "Why don't you raise up an altar instead of being preoccupied with the problems? Your worship will become an outpost of righteousness in the midst of a crooked and perverse world."

BUILD A NEW ALTAR WHEREVER YOU MOVE

After a length of time had passed, Abraham moved to the mountain between Bethel and Ai where he pitched his tent and built another an altar (see Genesis 12:8). For the first time, Scripture says, he also "called on the name of the LORD." It is significant that the Hebrew word *shem*, translated here as "name," also embraces the concept of God's *character*.

By calling upon God's character, Abraham's prayers entered a new dimension of intimacy with the Almighty. In Abraham's time, God was just beginning to rework His communication with fallen humanity. Abraham answered God's call because he believed there was a true and living God in the midst of the pagan culture around him. He sensed God drawing his heart to a promise of something that he could not be in himself, and at each new place of worship encounter, Abraham called on the character of the Lord.

In the same regard, it is important for us to consecrate a new home to the Lord with praise and worship before moving in. We have no way of knowing what took place there before we arrived. Even if it is a house or apartment that has never been lived in before, we have no idea what was going on while it was being built. Wherever you move, lift up an altar to the Lord, and take your rightful possession of the property.

Shortly after I came to pastor The Church On The Way, our family moved into a house that had previously been lived in by Christians. At that time we did not have the understanding we have now and were probably lulled into a false sense of security by the fact that the previous owners had been believers. After about five weeks of living there, my wife, Anna, and I were up in the middle of a night with a sick child when it suddenly occurred to me that some member of our family had been sick ever since we had moved there. As I thought about it, it struck me abruptly that the previous owners had told us that when their son returned from Vietnam, he had been on drugs, and they had had all sorts of problems with him and his drug-taking friends. Although it was about three o'clock in the morning, we got up and went through the house, room by room, asking the Lord to show us how to pray in each room. After that, the sickness was completely broken in our family.

Raising up a new altar of worship to the Lord whenever we move will sanctify our new dwelling place and put out a clean, spiritual "welcome mat" for His blessings and protection.

RENEW THE ALTAR

On returning from Egypt, Abraham went back to Bethel and renewed the altar he had built there (see Genesis 13:3–4). He repeated the process and re-established worship in his home. Abraham was not just going through repetitions of ritualism—his true worship invited a *rekindling* of God's presence.

On occasion, it is good for us to renew the commitments we have made to the Lord, especially as they relate to our families. I remember one particular time when the Lord woke me in the middle of the night and moved me to pray for each of my children. Anna and I were not having problems with our kids; it was just that something needed to be rekindled in each one of them. Over the next 48 hours, in direct response to specific things that I had prayed for each of them, the Lord touched them in a very natural way and worked a revival in our family. A renewing comes upon a household in which people praise and worship the Lord, declaring, "There is room for God in our house."

WALK THE LAND

At the fourth encounter along Abraham's journey, the Lord showed him a place, made him a promise and told him to take a prophetic action—to "walk the land." Abraham responded by building another altar at which to worship. God told him:

> "Lift your eyes now and look from the place where you are— northward, southward, eastward, and westward; for all the land which you see I give to you and your descendants forever. And I will make your descendants as the dust of the earth; so that if a man could number the dust of the earth, then your descendants also could be numbered. Arise, walk in the land through its length and its width, for I give it to you." Then Abram . . . built an altar there to the LORD.
>
> Genesis 13:14–18

Why would God tell Abraham to "walk the land" if in the same breath He told him that He was going to give it to him anyway? God was not wasting words or playing games. He was moving Abraham from ethereal, intangible notions to solid, faith-securing convictions. Building altars inescapably links the idea of God's *promise* to *prophetic action*— action taken in the physical, visible realm because of something we believe about the spiritual, invisible realm. Such action moves beyond the *idea* of God's promise to the *conviction* that His promise is in action—*now*.

The altar that Abraham built represents direction in his life that moved him another step forward toward possessing his destiny. Given a promise of future possession, Abraham acted *then* as the possessor and built an altar to commemorate the act.

We have every right, according to the victory won by our Savior Jesus Christ, who secured God's promise to us, to walk the land where we live and, in worship, to re-establish boundaries—to declare our "land" (wherever we are and wherever we go) to be under the dominion and blessing of God and His Kingdom.

There is a real place in the life of the contemporary Spirit-filled believer today for rediscovering the unalterable need for altars. Altars are thresholds—the footings of a doorway—for the entry of heaven's power and God's grace to pour forth into our lives and our world. God meets us where—and wherever—we worship Him. Altars mark those places as the milestones of our walk with Him and the prophetic action that welcomes His promise. The Lord was able to fulfill His promise to Abraham because Abraham made worship the center of his life.

His promise to you and me is nothing less.

1. The name of Abram, which means "Exalted Father," is changed to Abraham ("Father of a Multitude") in Genesis 17:5.

CHAPTER 10

With Voices Loud and High

The Song of Worship

Then the Levites . . . stood up to praise the LORD God of Israel with voices loud and high.

2 Chronicles 20:19

Nothing is more basic to our worship practices than song, but there is possibly nothing more dynamically significant to it either. Apart from the Word of God itself, singing constitutes more than a pivotal part of our gatherings—it is the most significant.

The Psalms depict this, indicating by their very existence the huge priority God puts upon "song" as a worship exercise of His people. I have often had people raise the question, "Pastor Jack, you speak about so many practices of worship—singing, praise, physical expressions, etc. Where do you find this in the guidelines to the New Testament Church?" The answer, of course, is the Psalms, which abound with directives, commands and biblical evidence for the practice of worshiping God. Even if there were not *one* New Testament reference to the details for God's order in our pursuit of worship, in the Psalms we would have all we need to answer the question. *The book of Psalms* was *the worship guide for early New Testament believers!* The New Testament, however, does contain more than fifteen references to song and singing, so there is no question regarding its place in the Church today.

The Lord has given His Church song not only as a powerful means by which His name may be extolled, but that thereby we may issue a welcomed entry of His ruling power into our midst. Without cheapening the concept of God's readiness to manifest Himself to His people, or suggesting He is dependent upon our song for His strength, it is not exaggerative to suggest that our songs of worship are a declarative "love song" of the Bride to the heavenly Bridegroom. In response, He rises in strength and with vigor to move among His people.

Whether we are gathered together by the thousands, or alone in our own homes, our song becomes our calling card—announcing, "Come here, Lord, as we seek You with our praise." His response is sure, as His own Word says He is "seeking" people who will worship Him in Spirit and in truth (see John 4). So we sometimes say, "Song introduces the rule of God's Kingdom and the dominion of His power," not that it generates that power, nor that our actions mandate His response. Rather, it becomes a learned principle, because open, song-filled, genuinely worshiping hearts are found by this God who seeks us. We discover from repeated experience that He *does* manifest Himself among people who wholeheartedly worship with "psalms and hymns and spiritual songs," as we "sing and make melody in our hearts to the Lord" (see Ephesians 5:19). Worked out in the experience of our daily lives, song becomes a powerful means of sustenance, triumph and ongoing growth in the Lord.

THE GIFT OF SONG

Human beings stand apart from all other creatures by the gifts of self-initiated speech and song bestowed only upon us. By creative capacity, our tongues are able to speak and to sing; no other creature can do that. We may speak of birds singing, but as lovely as that it is, birdsong is not consciously generated singing, and thus *song* as we are discussing it. Only humankind creates new songs and links them to consciously created lyrics that express more than a mere animal response of a natural endowment.

David expressly refers in three of the psalms to his speech and song-giving capacity, as well as his tongue, as his "glory" (Psalm 16:9; 30:12; 57:8). The word *glory* essentially means "to excel beyond." Man excels beyond every other creature by our capacity for song.

Instruction in the songs of the Lord during David's reign released God's power and brought forth His victory. That same victory is intended for God's people today: Song thus becomes, for many including myself, easily acknowledged as one of the "keys of the Kingdom of God" with which Jesus endows His Church (see Matthew 16:19). As keys ignite or provide access, song ignites hearts and accesses possibilities in praise that welcome and experience the release of Jesus' life and power among His people.

Let's look at 1 Chronicles 25:1–8 as an example of the way that song was prioritized under the leadership of King David. Note verse 1: "Moreover David and the captains of the army separated for the service some of the sons of Asaph, of Heman, and of Jeduthun, who should prophesy with harps, stringed instruments, and cymbals."

David established a new place in Israel's life for the use of and permanent valuing of song in worship. He set up companies of singers whose job was to praise the Lord, and the Holy Spirit blessed that arrangement. David knew from his own experience that an "anointing" may come upon worshipful singing. He sought means for others to be expressive in worship, and they, too, entered the arena of experiencing "anointing" through worshiping in song.

The Bible relates that the Holy Spirit came upon these musicians and singers, and they prophesied. In some cases it seems to have happened spontaneously during worship (see verse 3), while in others they prophesied "according to the order of the king" (verse 2). One entire family of musicians worked under the direction of their father for the music in the house of the Lord (see verse 6). All the musicians and singers were instructed in the song of the Lord under the authority of the king (see verse 7). This narrative seems to indicate almost inescapably that David did not institute music as essentially an artistic or aesthetic practice. He saw it as a prophetic music ministry—feeling a hunger himself for God's presence among His people, and recognizing that God wanted to visit His people, manifest His Spirit among them and move powerfully and personally among them as they worshiped Him in song.

As king and governing leader, as well as a psalmist and worshiper, David understood well the power of worship. And as we saw in chapter 8, there was a direct relationship between Israel's commitment to worship and the expansion of its territorial boundaries under his leadership.

Parallel to this, then, is to see that song is directed similarly in the early Church—woven into the fabric of its rapid expansion. Spiritual discernment and spiritual growth are increased through worshipful song. At Ephesus, it is directed as a part of openly receiving the wisdom of God (for discerning His will), and for maintaining a balanced, continuing fullness of the Holy Spirit:

> See then that you walk circumspectly, not as fools but as wise ... understand[ing] what the will of the Lord is ... [and keep on being] filled with the Spirit, speaking to one another in psalms and hymns and spiritual songs, singing and making melody in your heart to the Lord.
>
> Ephesians 5:15, 17–19

At Colosse, worshipful song is directly related to a believer's being open to and integrating God's living Word—in life and for spiritual profit: "Let the word of Christ dwell in you richly in all wisdom, teaching and admonishing one another in psalms and hymns and spiritual songs, singing with grace in your hearts to the Lord" (Colossians 3:16).

I have often wondered if the difference between merely rote learning of God's Word apart from an atmosphere of worship, and a complete integration of worshipful song with the teaching of Scripture might affect the way a believer "digests and assimilates" the bread, meat and milk of the Word for growth and health in Christ. That is, in the same way gastric juices in the tracts of the human body convert food to energy, so a healthy mix of song, praise and worship is essential to cultivating a people. They become not merely legal, literal "experts" of the Word, but submitted, worshiping singers of praise—whose song "breaks up" the spiritual content of God's Word and flows it into the heart, mind, soul and life.

These are ways it appears that the dwelling of God's presence and the dominion of His life and power are realized and released in worship-filled song.

SING WITH THE UNDERSTANDING

It is important that we recognize that our singing is not simply an acquired habit of church life. Psalm 47:6–7 (KJV) is explicit about this: "Sing praises to God, sing praises: sing praises unto our King, sing praises. For God is the King of all the earth: sing ye praises with understanding." It is a God-directed call, and if obeyed it yields God-ordained fruit. That is why I have pursued a goal of teaching people principles related to the power of song, seeking to overthrow any notion of either (1) that song is simply "a thing we do in church" or (2) that song is an optional point of participation. Truth taught about song in our worship, as well as in our private lives, moves believers to sing—to "sing with the understanding."

In at least 41 of the psalms we are told to sing praises to God, and in some, the injunction is repeated as many as three or four times. Singing is commanded; it has nothing to do with whether a person feels like singing or likes to sing. It is a fact that hosts of believers are reticent to sing in church, fearing their skill at it is not sufficient. But I urge people to get over it, saying, "God isn't operating a talent contest. He isn't grooming you for an 'American Idol' quest for fame." He is wanting to break down idols of pride that may secretly have found a place in our reserve. Every evidence of Scripture is that the Lord wants to bring a full flow of worshiping song from the lips of every one of His people; to hear us sing boldly, no matter the quality of our singing voices. Our sense of inadequacy, shaped by the world, causes us to draw comparisons with more gifted singers, but where the Lord is concerned, there is a particular beauty to everything He has created. There is no sound that is without significance to Him (see 1 Corinthians 14:10).

People who sing praise unabashedly see the glory of the Lord begin to break forth in their voices. If you have been restrained in this area, ask the Holy Spirit to make you an anointed singer of worshipful praise (even if you're never appointed as a soloist!).

The Applied Power of Song

Having engaged this body of biblical references to "song," I want to invite you to open your heart in a personal and practical way to the *applied* power of song as it was opened to my own understanding in Isaiah 54:1–5.

The truth of this passage became profoundly confirming to me after an experience of being moved to sing and shout praise by myself in our church sanctuary. I was moving with a sense of intercessory dynamic—as a means of penetrating a situation human hands could not affect, and giving place to songs "in the spirit and with the understanding" to make my intercession. I knew it was something I was supposed to do, but it was not until years later that I discovered a breakthrough principle—the power of song to overthrow oppression and barrenness. Read with me:

"Sing, O barren,
You who have not borne!
Break forth into singing, and cry aloud,
You who have not labored with child!
For more are the children of the desolate
Than the children of the married woman," says the LORD.

Isaiah 54:1

This passage of Scripture is the Lord's direction to a barren woman; the command to sing directly faces the problem of barrenness. First let me discuss this culturally, as it was viewed in Isaiah's day, and then personally, as it manifests in each of us in different ways. Then we will discover how power is released into our own situations when we understand the principle behind lifting our voices in worshipful song.

It is important for us to understand that in the culture of ancient Israel a barren woman was considered worthless. That was a terribly heartless assessment! This was not the Lord's view, of course, but it was society's view, and so far-reaching was it that a married woman who could not conceive could be divorced by her husband. At the very least she was made to feel totally useless and rejected. Her situation was hopeless. It was one of the grossest manifestations of chauvinism that can be imagined.

Into this situation of futility and hopelessness the Lord speaks. But what He says seems peculiar. He says to a woman who is facing humiliation and rejection, "Start singing!" And then He makes a promise: He says that her barrenness will not hinder her but that she will have children. In fact, He says, "More are the children of the desolate than the children of the married woman."

Once she is singing and has His promise to hold onto, the barren woman is exhorted to start getting ready by making room: "Enlarge the place of your tent, and let them stretch out the curtains of your dwellings; do not spare; lengthen your cords, and strengthen your stakes" (verse 2).

It is clear that the Lord is saying that a baby is coming and, as a matter of fact, since "you shall expand to the right and to the left" (verse 3), it is clear that there is more than one baby on its way. And to top it off, He talks about the fruitfulness that will come from those offspring.

The problem of barrenness is not confined to women unable to bear children, although their experience is uniquely painful. At times in everyone's life we all experience barrenness, when no life seems to be forthcoming and what life there is seems to miscarry. Perhaps there are people whom you long to see saved, but who are so deep in bondage to some addiction or to despair that you wonder how this might ever be achieved. Perhaps you have aspirations or dreams that you long to see fulfilled, and you wonder why these things have never come about. Barrenness is something that confronts all of us and afflicts us in different ways.

But remember God's word in Scripture to the barren woman: The problem of barrenness will be answered by a promise, and the principle that makes this a reality is song.

In other words, the call to *new life* is made via song.

Now that really does seem peculiar. We think that singing is just something we do. The Lord says that it is more than that; He tells us that there is *power* in song.

There are a number of places in the Bible besides Isaiah 54 that show the power and functional dynamic of song, including three worthy of detailed study:

1. The dialogue between the Lord and Job in which the text discloses that singing attended God's creation of

our world (see Job 38). This is the principle of *song relating to the creative power of God.*

2. The story of Jehoshaphat in 2 Chronicles 20 where the army is led into battle by the choir. This is the principle of *song bringing victory in battle.*

3. The dramatic deliverance of Paul and Silas from imprisonment in Philippi (see Acts 16). This is the principle of *song bringing release from bondage.*

Let's take each of these and evaluate the lessons they teach us about the power of worshipful song.

1. Song Accompanies God's Creative Power

Out of a whirlwind, the Lord declared Himself to Job, and it is in this encounter that we are introduced to a functional dynamic within song. The text discloses that singing attended God's creation of our world as the heavenly host began to swell with choruses of praise in recognition of the marvel and majesty of His power.

Reviewing the story of Job's dialogue with God, we discover how Job had the audacity to tell the Creator of the universe that he was not very pleased with the way He was conducting matters. In turn, the Lord said, in effect, "Okay, I have a couple of questions for you. If you can answer them, I'll start answering your charges." It is almost humorous to read how unaffectedly non-religious and direct that early saint's words were, and stunningly disarming to read God's gracious-but-confrontive response. God posed these questions to Job:

"Where were you when I laid the foundations of the earth?
Tell Me, if you have understanding.
Who determined its measurements?
Surely you know!...
To what were its foundations fastened?"

Job 38:4–6

In the midst of challenging Job about the whole creation process God said this: "Who laid its cornerstone, when the morning stars sang together, and all the sons of God shouted for joy?" (verses 6–7).

Pausing to meditate, we can see how God made His main point by asking Job about the creation of the earth: Where was Job when it took place? Who determined its boundaries? Who laid the cornerstone? But possibly the most compelling point of analysis for us is in a seemingly passing observation the Lord made amid these questions. God linked His actions in creating the earth to the singing of angelic choirs chorusing praise. In brief, we might broadly say, "God uses music as an accompaniment to His creative activity."

I might muse on this, semi-humorously: We all are aware of the mass availability today of music to exercise by, music to dine by and there may be, for all I know, music to tear out your crankcase by. So don't think it peculiar if I imagine something not irreverent, but certainly relevant; that in the timelessness of eternity, I conceive something of a scene like this. The Lord rises from His throne, turns to the heavenly hosts and says, "Guys, I'm going to do some creating today, so give Me a little background music!" Of course, that specific scenario is more than just a little unlikely, but still it is clear: Job's account confirms that when God began to create, there was a simultaneous rising of anthems of worship and praise by the heavenly hosts—

doubtless in wonder and in recognition of the marvel and majesty of His power.

The relationship between song and creativity is inescapable. One cannot help but wonder how often God takes the songs of worship wafted from prayer warriors interceding in their prayer closets, and sets in motion miracles of His "new creation" workings! Don't think it a stretch, dear one. When you are calling on the Lord for things unimaginable—things needing His creative workings—sing!

Incidentally, such a view is not unique to my imagination, as many of you who are familiar with C. S. Lewis's Chronicles of Narnia will be aware. In these masterful works written for children by a man who was both an intellectual genius and a serious Bible scholar, Lewis depicts the great lion Aslan (a clearly intended picture of the Person of Christ) creating the land of Narnia by singing it into existence. I have little reason to doubt that Lewis conceived this idea by reason of this passage in the book of Job.

This notation in Scripture is not just a matter of poetic license; I think it is a point of revelation. Song goes side by side with victory, release, creation and other actions noted in the Bible. The life-begetting power of song has all kinds of implications when it comes to things you and I routinely face that seem to be at a standstill.

The Power of Song to Confront Barrenness

I remember clearly one occasion, as I was preaching on Isaiah 54:1–5 soon after the Lord had brought these truths alive to me, when an unusual thing took place. In only one of the four services that weekend, I felt profoundly prompted by the Holy Spirit to speak a prophetic word of faith to couples present in that service who had not been able to conceive. I did not ask them to identify themselves, but simply said, "Even though I have not been moved to apply this Scripture directly to physical barrenness in other services this weekend, I feel the Lord has pressed a word of prophecy into my spirit. As you have heard me teach, my focus has been on the unproductive areas of our lives, or places where barricades obstruct the way. But I sense there is a more direct call of the Spirit in this service; that there are people here who are to be encouraged to believe and to begin to sing as was the woman in this text: The Lord is calling, 'Sing, O barren . . .' and there will be children."

The confirmation of that word of the Spirit was remarkably wonderful. In the course of the next two years, we dedicated babies from two couples in our church family who had been unable to conceive for seven years in one case and ten years in the other! Each couple told me that they had been in that service, and that following it they had begun to worship regularly together, filling their homes with song—embracing the witness of promise the Holy Spirit had given them.

In this passage of Scripture, through the prophet Isaiah, God teaches us how to address those barren situations into which we have not seen His life or power enter: We are to sing over them. One way to do this is to come before the Lord in prayer and simply name our family members, friends or heretofore fruitless situations, saying something like, "Lord, I bring John to You" or "Lord, I bring Sally" or "Lord, this situation is such a wreck." And then, simply holding the issues before the Lord in prayer, begin to sing. We can sing with the understanding or we can sing with the Spirit. In this way we give recognition to the truth that the power of song has been given to us to confront barrenness.

The Power of Song to Restore and Release

In discussing the power of song, be assured that I am not proposing that singing is a magic method to make miracles happen. The Sovereign Lord is the One who alone exercises the power and chooses to move among us. But it is also clear that He has chosen to relate to us in love and through the power of His Holy Spirit who delights in all glorifying and magnifying of Jesus. So there is reason to believe that our praise to God and His Son, lifted up in song, does have something to do with our partnering role with Him in seeing the release of His desired purposes on earth and in our midst.

Accordingly, in applying the power of song, there may be occasions when we sing and find no corresponding release point—for example, barrenness may continue to prevail. But this may well indicate not an ineffectively applied principle, but an incomplete response of our own souls to Him *in another matter*. It may be that God is delaying the answer in order that character, for example, might be developed within us. Another story from the life of our church will explain what I mean.

About three years after the prophetic word I mentioned giving, a young woman came to me at her husband's request. She was not unkind or ungracious to me, but she was disturbed, and I could sense bitter anger in her heart. Like the other couples, she and her husband had been unable to conceive. She had heard the series of messages I had given on the subject, and she and her husband had sung together over their situation. But nothing had happened. She tried to cover up her distress, but the question was wrung from her heart: "Why don't I have a baby?"

I didn't know what to say to her.

Although I was aware that this could sound like the world's worst cop-out, I suggested that perhaps the Lord had a redemptive purpose in wanting them to adopt a child. She explained to me that she was not opposed to this possibility, yet through her tears, she also told me of a deep longing for her own child.

And I hurt for her.

At least two more years went by, and then we had the joy of dedicating a child that she bore. Although she never said so in so many words, I think she recognized that God needed to purge some bitterness out of her system and had delayed the answer to her prayers for this purpose.

It wasn't that God was being loveless toward her in the meantime. The Lord does not just answer our songs for new life and blessing for the purpose of saying, "Here's a little goodie for you," like a heavenly Santa Claus passing out lollipops. The Lord is bringing us into the fulfillment of His purpose. Oftentimes the greatest grace and mercy is that which requires the development of our character before the manifestation of His kindness that we are hoping for. Not that our character growth earns something; rather, whatever is poisoning us is resolved.

This passage of Scripture also points us to another great truth about how our attitudes can affect His response:

> "Do not fear, for you will not be ashamed;
> Neither be disgraced, for you will not be put to shame;
> For you will forget the shame of your youth,
> And will not remember the reproach of your widowhood
>   anymore."
>
> Isaiah 54:4

This verse begins by saying, "Do not fear." Why in the face of the wonderful promise God has just made about enlarging the place of one's tent would anyone be afraid? Because every one of us is vulnerable to the accusation that our pasts disqualify us from any expectation that such a wonderful promise could be fulfilled. We are ashamed and afraid. Can you imagine someone—yourself?—starting to sing in a place that needs a flow of new life and the voice of fears creeps in: *What if I am just making sounds? Just whistling in the dark? What if this is a song in the night, and there is never going to be a dawn? It's too late. I missed it.*

God's Word tells us, in effect, "Don't be afraid. Don't succumb to the lie that says you are only being teased or that you have conned yourself into hoping for something that really isn't My promise." He encourages you and me, just as He did the barren woman: "You will not be put to shame. You will forget the shame of your youth. Start to sing, because the shame of your past is not going to be a hindrance to what I am going to do."

God can make up for our lost time. Remember His words through the prophet Joel: "I will restore to you the years that the swarming locust has eaten, the crawling locust, the consuming locust, and the chewing locust" (Joel 2:25).

If we will call upon God's power in song, we will not be abandoned and we will not be put to shame. Our pasts will not disqualify us from the restoration He plans for the barrenness in our lives. He will restore those lost and lonely years.

The climax of the text comes in Isaiah 54:5 where God describes Himself: "For your Maker is your husband, the LORD of hosts is His name; and your Redeemer is the Holy One of Israel; He is called the God of the whole earth."

As our Maker, He is able to create anything that is needful for our lives. As our Redeemer, He is able to restore, to gather back whatever is lost. As the God of the whole earth, there is nothing that He cannot rule or overrule.

As we lift our songs of worship, He releases His concern and power for us. In our personal lives, in our work, in our families, in our actual wombs, as we sing of the almightiness of God, He releases power to our personal points of barrenness. He is our Creator, Restorer, Ruler, Savior. And He says, "Sing!"

2. Song Leads to Victory in Battle

The most well-known story of a decisive battle won through the power of song is found in 2 Chronicles 20. The stance of faith that sent the choir of Judah marching in front of the army onto the battlefield unfolds a wonderful lesson about the interface of worship and warfare. This is the story of a people whose national life was threatened and who faced tremendous confrontation—even potential extinction. Through worship, victory in a life-or-death struggle was accomplished.

Jehoshaphat, King of Judah, grew fearful as he received word that the nations around him were amassing for attack. Can you see yourself in this picture? The enemy comes marching in on people in their life-circumstances and says, "It's all going to be over for you at a certain time." Such things occur to believers everywhere: A terminal diagnosis concerning a person's health . . . a negative prognosis on family finances . . . the threat of an ultimatum in a troubled marriage. In the face of those things, we are wise to look at Jehoshaphat as he faced his "ultimatum." His response models for us how to sing when you are struggling for your life. Our reaction to dire circumstances—whether of faith or of fear—will determine the outcome.

Jehoshaphat's initial reaction of fear in the face of sudden crisis did not disqualify him as a person of faith or as a person of potential victory. In short, simply pretending a denial of fear does not qualify a person as "spiritual." But what does make the difference is what we do—what any person does—when fear strikes. Look at Jehoshaphat's course of action: His first line of defense and answer to fear was to seek the Lord with a fast (see verse 3). Like any wise believer, he doubtless knew that fasting is a not a means by which we bargain with God or somehow "earn" His interest. Fasting is an instrument of spiritual warfare— an instrument by which demonic, satanic powers are weakened and eventually broken (see Daniel 9–10). In declaring the fast throughout Judah, King Jehoshaphat recognized that the battle was essentially spiritual; that forces marshaled by a people who worshiped another god were seeking to overthrow the worship and reduce the apparent worthiness of the God of Israel.

In Paul's words, "We do not wrestle against flesh and blood, but against [demonic opposition]" (Ephesians 6:12). Too often we make our counterattack in the energy of the flesh rather than in the power of the Spirit. How many people try to figure out ways to deal with the physical expression of the problem, rather than cutting right to the source—the spiritual root? Attacks against us are often based on the enterprises of hell seeking to discredit or dissolve the effectiveness of the purposes of God in and through His people.

Jehoshaphat confronted a physical reality with a spiritual dynamic—fasting and worship—and the Spirit of the Lord responded. The people prayed and in the midst of their worship, the Spirit of God came upon Jahaziel, a recognized prophet:

> "Thus says the LORD to you. 'Do not be afraid nor dismayed because of this great multitude, for the battle is not yours, but God's. Tomorrow go down against them.... You will not need to fight in this battle. Position yourselves, stand still and see the salvation of the LORD, who is with you, O Judah and Jerusalem!' Do not fear or be dismayed; tomorrow go out against them, for the LORD is with you."
>
> 2 Chronicles 20:15–17

In response to the prophetic word of the Lord the people bowed in worship again:

> And Jehoshaphat bowed his head with his face to the ground, and all Judah and the inhabitants of Jerusalem bowed before the LORD, worshiping the LORD. Then the Levites of the children of the Kohathites and of the children of the Korahites stood up to praise the LORD God of Israel with voices loud and high.
>
> verses 18–19

The Lord still speaks to people through the prophetic prompting of the Spirit. Prophetic utterance, while not equated with Scripture, must be supported by Scripture. People may discount the present ministry of the Holy Spirit, but God has spoken to all of us at one time or another about our lives; and we need to make up our minds whether or not we will receive the word the Lord gives to our hearts.

This prophetic word, no doubt, encouraged them the next day when they actually had to face the enemy. We have all had the experience of waking up the next morning to see our faith beginning to evaporate as a problem still presents itself. But as Jehoshaphat "consulted" with the people (see verse 21), probably to review God's prophetic promise to them the day before, faith took action. The choir's decision? March out with singing and praises to God. As worship went forth, confusion came over Judah's enemies. Their adversaries turned against one another and destroyed themselves. It took three days to collect the spoils.

The choir's choice to go before the army was not a ruse: It reflected their conviction. They had seen their king on his knees, as Jehoshaphat declared (1) The Lord is God above all, (2) His power is beyond all, and (3) there is nothing that can come upon His people that He cannot handle (see verses 6–12). Their song was a full-orbed recognition of who was going before them! So as the choir advanced with their song, moving toward the battle, they did so with confidence in the Lord, who by His servant had prophesied that He would fight for them! Their faith, revealed in the action joined to their worship, was based on the Word of God—on the proven record of His history of working deliverance when His people call out to Him.

Faith comes by hearing, and by knowing the certainty of the Word of God. It contains the recorded, redemptive history of how God acts, and presents the promise that His character has not changed—He is still the same today, and responds to His people now just as He did in the past.

We all come to our time to decide, Is this true? Can the power of God's promise truly be appropriated—faith be stimulated—as I worship and seek Him? Will He do for me when I sing, what He did for Jehoshaphat and his people?

I think the answer is in God's Word. Faith begins to rise when we come out of a solid view that God is faithful, unchanging, and that not one word of His good promise has failed (see Joshua 23:14).

When it looks as though everything is mounted against us and our future is washed up, our victorious response ought to be like that of Jehoshaphat's:

- Seek God first.
- Allow your faith to grow by recounting the history of God's work.
- Listen to the Holy Spirit as He speaks to you.
- Proceed, worshiping with a faith-evoked song.

Through our worship, the Lord will win the battle for us.

3. Song Brings Release from Bondage

David wrote in Psalm 32:7: "You are my hiding place; You shall preserve me from trouble; You shall surround me with songs of deliverance. Selah."

A striking and dramatic demonstration of the power of worship not only to bring deliverance, but also to pave the way for evangelism is seen in Acts 16 when Paul and Silas were imprisoned at Philippi. The song of the Lord shook the powers of darkness and released a family and ultimately a city, a continent and an entire hemisphere:

> But at midnight Paul and Silas were praying and singing hymns to God, and the prisoners were listening to them. Suddenly there was a great earthquake, so that the foundations of the prison were shaken; and immediately all the doors were opened and everyone's chains were loosed. And the keeper of the prison, awaking from sleep and seeing the prison doors open, supposing the prisoners had fled, drew his sword and was about to kill himself. But Paul called with a loud voice, saying, "Do yourself no harm, for we are all

here." Then he called for a light, ran in, and fell down trembling before Paul and Silas. And he brought them out and said, "Sirs, what must I do to be saved?" So they said, "Believe on the Lord Jesus Christ, and you will be saved, you and your household." Then they spoke the word of the Lord to him and to all who were in his house. And he took them the same hour of the night and washed their stripes. And immediately he and all his family were baptized.

verses 25–33

To my mind, this episode stands as a profound case for the power of song. I cannot see Paul's and Silas's singing as simply an effort at cheering themselves through a dark hour. Rather, I believe that as the men of spiritual, biblical insight that they were, they knew and applied this principle. So, in the face of gargantuan obstacles—(1) incarceration, (2) political resistance, (3) the quest to plant a church in a pagan city, and (4) the pursuit of penetrating the continent of Europe with the Gospel—they sang.

They did not do this simply because they had no other recourse, but because they knew the exaltation of the Most High gives place to His sovereign and gracious purposes—to His manifest presence. "The Lord GOD of hosts ... touches the earth and it melts" (Amos 9:5). I am not suggesting either, that the jailed worshipers expected an earthquake, or that every earthquake is the result of worship. I am expressing the conviction that those two singers knew the power of worship, exercised it in the middle of an almost impossibly blockaded mission and the result was (1) their liberation, (2) favor with the authorities, (3) prevention of a suicide, conversion of a jailer, bringing salvation to his household, and (4) a planted church and a penetrated continent. *Worship is a key to breakthrough evangelism.*

SINGING IN THE SPIRIT

It is unusually significant to my mind, that the gigantic intellect so obviously present in the apostle Paul is so uninhibited in describing his own employment of the benefits of both praying in and singing "in the Spirit" (see 1 Corinthians 14:13–20). His letter to the Corinthian church, for instance, seeks clearly to correct confusing misapplications of the benefits of spiritual language among the congregation, but in it he unashamedly asserts his own currency and practice of the same. Paul is essentially saying, "If you employ 'speaking with tongues' insensitively, they become distracting. If you employ them as I have learned to, you will find them personally edifying" (see 14:4).

There is no way that the phrase "I will sing with the Spirit" can mean anything else in this context other than to sing "in tongues"—to employ the Holy Spirit-given capacity for spiritual language (glossolalia). This gains added reinforcement in both passages in which Paul exhorts New Testament believers to worship with "songs, hymns and spiritual songs" (see Ephesians 5:19; Colossians 3:16). The Greek words *hodais pneumatikais* (spiritual songs) use the same word for "spiritual" that is used in 1 Corinthians 14:1, introducing the subject of the gifts of the Holy Spirit. In other words, we are again faced with Paul's very natural and affirming reference to a practical, prayerful or worshipful employment of speaking with tongues in the private, devotional life of a believer.

For those who may not be familiar with it, the subject of spiritual language was introduced by Jesus Himself: "And these signs will follow those who believe: In My name they will . . . speak with new tongues" (Mark 16:17).

Speaking with "new tongues" is the first of five signs revealed in this text that Jesus Himself prophesied would be common among His redeemed. Today, wherever fears are dissolved through a faithful teaching of the truth of God's Word on this subject, speaking with tongues becomes almost universally experienced. Contrary to the idea that "tongues" is a fanatical "trip," the blessing of the Holy Spirit's expansion of our capacity for private praise and worship is wonderfully fulfilling and liberating. It is the Spirit's answer to Charles Wesley's heart-cry voiced in his hymn,

> O for a thousand tongues to sing my great Redeemer's
>   praise,
> The glories of my God and King, the triumphs of His grace!

The ability to worship and praise God at a new, transcendent dimension was manifested on the very day the Church was born:

> And they were all filled with the Holy Spirit and began to speak with other tongues, as the Spirit gave them utterance ... [to which those hearing responded that] "we hear them speaking in our own tongues the wonderful works of God."
>
> Acts 2:4, 11

Some of you who have already received your spiritual language may not have been taught that you are also called and free to express it in song. In my own journey with Jesus, my first exposure to this privilege was not without its own beauty, but I still found myself reluctant to "sing with the Spirit." The non-rhythmic, simple placement of words upon a sustained tone that rises or falls or a tune that the singer innovates for himself was strangely threatening to me. Even though I *wrote* music, and even though I already prayed daily in my spiritual language as well as in English, the "new" was a stretch for me. More honestly, I was having to come to terms with pride—with that human preference to have things on my own terms. But I remember once hearing a pastor say, "When's the last time you did anything for the first time in Jesus' name?" The question confronted my reserve.

I chose to "sing with the Spirit"—to obey the directive of Scripture, and I found it was infinitely easier to do than one may think. I have found, in fact, that if people simply begin by singing praise—glorifying Jesus, singing "Hallelujah"— that once they do, they often discover that singing with the Spirit is probably the most natural way of praising God. We can begin with a known melody and then launch out on our own. (If you have not yet received a release of Holy Spirit-enabled prayer or spiritual language, and you believe God's Word that His promise of the Holy Spirit's fullness and benefits are the same for you as for those early believers [see Acts 2:38–39], simply ask the Holy Spirit to overflow you with new dimensions of worship, in Jesus' name. If you wish to consult it, a prayer to receive the fullness of the Holy Spirit has been placed in Appendix 2.)

Song Is a Key to the Kingdom

The relationship between song and creativity is inescapable. Song is not just an incidental or liturgical part of our worship; it is a key to the Kingdom that releases God's life-begetting flow into our world and our lives. Song is a natural means of uniting together: It is a beautiful means of praise and worship, and a powerful means of challenging darkness and declaring the truth.

Few things delight God's heart more than when we lift words of worship and praise to Him in song. As we sing, declaring the truth of God's goodness, rehearsing the assurance of His victory and praising His capacity to create and beget life, we become enabled by His Spirit to confront what would seek to quench or hinder. When we worship God in song, the power of darkness—in every area of our lives and in every circumstance in our world—is challenged. The power of song hastens the coming of His Kingdom "on earth as it is in heaven." Begin to sing in your devotional times, when you are driving alone in the car, when you are out for a walk. Let your praises of our wondrous Lord and Savior rise in song: *"Sing, O barren!"* and *life* shall spring forth.

And as was promised to the barren one, the power inherent in song holds God's promise for you and me—one that invites us all to expect new boundaries of blessing: "For you shall expand to the right and to the left, and your descendants will inherit the nations"(Isaiah 54:3).

And therein lies the objective of all worship—to glorify God who delights to birth life as well as to overflow life until it touches every land and people.

Let's not simply "go for it"! Let's lift our voices loud and high with the life-begetting power of song, and let us sing until the nations are won to His Son!

CHAPTER 11

Shouting "Grace!"
and Saying "Amen"

The Affirmation of Worship

Throughout the Bible, we are reminded in both positive and negative terms of the power of our words. James tells us, "Even so the tongue is a little member and boasts great things" (3:5). What falls from our lips is pivotal when it comes to the victory (or fumbling) of our walk with the Lord, particularly as that relates to our worship. Our words open (or close off) the pathway for God's power and Kingdom authority to enter our personal world. Just as we have examined at length the power of song, let me invite you to think with me regarding two further expressions common to our worship.

154

No song is more common to worship at a global dimension than the beloved and truth-filled simplicity in the hymn "Amazing Grace." We preach God's grace, we believe in God's grace and the word occurs over and over in our song and hymnody. And it is in the light of the possibility that we are all ever-vulnerable to "knowing something so well or hearing something so often we forget the depth of its reality and wonder," that I want you to traverse an Old Testament story with me—one about *grace*; about *shouting* "Grace!"

Another word that occurs so regularly in our worship gatherings we are inclined to regard it as a mere formality, or as a mere affirmation spoken by an excited listener, is the word *Amen*. Driven by the conviction that *those worship most effectively who think clearly as they seek God humbly* I suggest we look at "Amen" and "Grace" as more than a worthwhile digression. I ask you to see these words as I have come to see them: as issues related to worship.

SHOUTING "GRACE!"

It is a characteristic of human beings to fall back on our own resourcefulness and self-propelled power rather than seek a release of God's grace to meet the challenges and obstacles that confront and confound us. But building a life of discipleship means depending upon what God has done and allowing His works to grow in our lives, rather than trying to rely upon human will, wisdom or strength. As a refreshing review, or as a stirring reminder of how we may each find lifelong experiences of release through God's grace, look with me at one Old Testament leader who faced staggering obstacles while trying to achieve the task to which God had called him.

Zerubbabel was the leader of fifty thousand exiles who were returning from Babylon. Those whom he led were, for the most part, the children and grandchildren of the Israelites who had been taken when Nebuchadnezzar had razed Jerusalem to the ground decades earlier. Very few of those captured would have survived, and so it was their descendants who made the return journey home.

Upon their return, the Israelites set about the task of rebuilding the Temple, at first with great zeal. But their initial enthusiasm began to wane as the daunting obstacles to accomplishing the task came into focus. The resources available to them were limited. Opposition from the neighboring Samaritans brought about an order from the then-reigning government to halt construction. Pre-occupation with other pursuits drained their energies. And amid these distractions, the few who had survived the term of captivity compared the goal of their efforts unfavorably to the former greatness and splendor of Solomon's Temple. All these things conspired to breed discouragement among the people. Their labors seemed worth so little, were taking so long and were so staunchly opposed.

It was at this low point in morale, in lost vision and in waning success with the building project that the prophet Zechariah gave an encouraging word to Zerubbabel. It is an intensely practical case to study, for it presents a word of divine counsel and action that speaks to those points of discouragement and stalled progress that so commonly impact our own lives. Zerubbabel was about to be led to a promise of God's intervening power, but it was hinged upon his response to a specific action that would be some-thing like a light-switch; it would "turn on the power" of God's grace.

"This is the word of the LORD to Zerubbabel:
'Not by might nor by power, but by My Spirit,'
Says the LORD of hosts.
'Who are you, O great mountain?
Before Zerubbabel you shall become a plain!
And he shall bring forth the capstone
With shouts of "Grace, grace to it!"' "

Moreover the word of the LORD came to me, saying:

"The hands of Zerubbabel
Have laid the foundation of this temple;
His hands shall also finish it.
Then you will know
That the LORD of hosts has sent Me to you."

Zechariah 4:6–9

God told Zerubbabel that it was not by human might, power, manipulation or intelligence that the battle would be won, but *by His Spirit*. The source of promise and power is always the same: All power belongs to God! But let me advance the analogy I mentioned a moment ago.

All the power that energizes the electrical systems of my house has a source beyond my ability to produce. It is generated elsewhere and "piped" via complex grids and wiring systems until it finally connects to Anna's and my home. The power comes from above, literally. Rain fills rivers; rivers fill dams; dams feed generators; generators direct electric power through wires. And when it arrives at our house, nothing works until I turn on a switch. Similarly, the power of God's grace must be accessed by decisive action.

In that light, let us continue with Zerubbabel, but allow me to place it in the context of our lives with these words: Jesus gives grace to His people when our lives are bogged down.

I want to invite each worshiper reading these words to think of the times your own worship is invaded by preoccupation with present difficulties. It isn't that you don't believe God is greater: It is just that faith somehow seems smaller—at least, as with Zerubbabel—faith for the completion of a task, vision or fulfillment of a God-given dream.

Perhaps there is a project that you had hoped to see completed that has gotten stuck, delayed or just never seems to get off the ground. You have tried everything you could to move it along only to have one thing after another get in the way until discouragement has finally settled in. The very sight of its unfinished state stands as a mockery to your witness and conviction that it be completed. This is how Zerubbabel felt as he surveyed the rebuilding of the Temple.

Yet God works by His grace in ways that are impossible for us to figure out; His summons to us, as it was to Zerubbabel, is that we call upon Him to release it.

Years ago, one of the greatest miracles to occur in Anna's and my life together took place at a time when we were a young couple trying to plant a church in a city where we knew no one. Our call to this mission was one we believed in, but it seemed it was about to be bogged down and dragged to a stop for want of funds. It will seem pitifully small to a reader today, but more than forty years ago—and given our situation—we were stumped because of our lack of $75. It may as well have been $75,000! It was at least as big for us as that "mountain" that Zerubbabel faced: "Who are you, O great mountain? Before Zerubbabel you shall become a plain! And he shall bring forth the capstone with shouts of 'Grace, grace to it!'" (verse 7).

We were well into the month of January. Christmas was past, and we knew any cash gifts we might likely receive from relatives or friends had already been given. Every human resource was dried up, a baby daughter and another child on the way presented a specter of economic futility, and neither Anna nor I could think of any possible source from which the money could come.

So well can I remember that day, as we knelt by the kitchen table. I said, "Honey, let me pray what I feel in my heart." She agreed with me as I said, "Lord, You are the One we trust, and we are thankful to be in so helpless a position. I want to ask this favor—this grace of You. Somewhere, Jesus, You know someone who has $75 who could send it to us. Would you speak to the person's heart to do that? We will praise You whatever happens, but this is our request."

What happened is as incredible a thing as has happened in my life. I have led a congregation through challenges to multi-million-dollar victories, but the $75 one is still an unforgotten wonder.

Four days later we received a check from a person we had never heard of in our lives and one whom none of our friends knew: It was for $75!

We had told no one of our plight. The check had no accompanying note, and to this day I have no idea how this individual knew about us or our situation. I wrote a letter to the person whose name was on the check, expressing our interest in knowing how the gift had come about. We never heard a word. God remained the only explanation—God's grace the only reason we had any recourse to hope.

I retell that simple story because God's promise to Zerubbabel is still the same: "Not by might [no contact or clout to stir action] nor by power [no dynamic of human strength or capacity], but by My Spirit."

Grace! The New Testament's favorite word for the Holy Spirit's working:

- *Charis*—the Greek word for "grace"—describing divine favor and the release of divine power in situations of human disability and undeservedness.
- *Charis*—the word used describing the miracles that began to flow from Stephen's life, as the Holy Spirit did works beyond human capacities (see Acts 6:8). Note: Some translations mistranslate *charis* and print "faith" rather than "grace."
- *Charis*—the first half of the word *charismata*, which refers to the gifts of the Holy Spirit and brings about operational displays of God's wisdom, knowledge, discernment, insight, power, healing, etc.—by His power alone (see 1 Corinthians 12).

There was nothing I could have possibly done to initiate the tremendous release of grace that came from God through this individual and met us at the point of our need other than going before Him in helplessness to ask. That is exactly where Zerubbabel was in his situation, but the Lord had spoken: "Oh great mountain—you will be leveled!"

God promises that life's "mountains"—obstacles that rise intimidatingly in our way—will be flattened out, not by our power but by His. And the words of Zechariah to Zerubbabel were clear: That mountain-moving power would come by the working of the Holy Spirit.

The word of prophetic promise to Zerubbabel was that he would "bring forth the capstone"—that is, the completion of the building project. In ancient times, the capstone was the last stone to be put in place—it was the finishing touch. As the keystone in an arch is the primary piece that assures not only completion but also endurance—if it is removed the whole arch will collapse—so Zerubbabel's building project would be finalized and secured as complete with the capstone. In essence, God was speaking to Zerubbabel by the prophet Zechariah as the two men stood on the building site surveying the half-completed Temple. And God said, "You *will* bring this Temple building to completion, but it won't by achieved by the power of human engineering."

How then? Zechariah declares the word of the Lord: "You will bring forth the capstone with shouts of 'Grace, grace to it!'"

It isn't hard to picture that capstone, already carved and fitted for its final placement, but lying on the ground there on the building site—readied for completion of a temple that seemed beyond expectation. Whenever Zerubbabel would walk by it, one can imagine feelings of uncertainty—the finest leaders have them. But God was speaking into his uncertainty, and with a peculiar command—a command to *shout* a repeated declaration of "Grace! Grace!"—an act that *the prophet said God said* would call forth the working of the Holy Spirit.

Just as Zerubbabel was building a temple, so readers of these words are engaged in building:

- You may be dismayed as you seek to build a marriage that isn't growing very well.
- You may be a pastor whose vision for the congregation seems to have bogged down.
- You may be a businessman whose enterprise has crawled to a near stopping point, and the red ink is beginning to flow.
- You may be wearied with a seeming impossible task or a recurrent failure in your pursuit as a believer.

Every one of us is part of a temple Jesus is building—His Church. It is not made by human hands, not out of brick, but out of people who are being built up as a spiritual house—a "dwelling place of God in the Spirit" (Ephesians 2:22). As individuals also, we are each a temple of the Lord (see 1 Corinthians 6:19), and the completion of God's purposes in us is remarkably parallel to the challenge Zerubbabel faced.

Whatever the case with any of us, not only is the message of the text wrapped in the truth that grace alone can suffice, but we are called to the humbling application of that truth—an open, bold commitment to announce, to declare our dependence on God—to shout at the obstacle, and in the name of the Lord and on the grounds of His promise, implore His Spirit's workings of grace!

I have brought this message on nearly every continent. I never end it without calling the people to imagine an exchange between Zechariah and Zerubbabel, in which the prophet calls the leader to an accountable response to the prophetic directive—to shout. First, I fix my appeal to make a response to the words of the text—affirming that the text says what it says, even if we want to dilute it to fit our own comfort zones. Second, I seek to enable a group response by singing, "Amazing Grace," and at its conclusion invite instruments to continue playing—suggesting that then, each person literally shout, declaring God's grace and the release of His Spirit, virtually firing the words at whatever obstacle they face in their lives.

People do that. And testimonies have come from around the world that as worshipers honor God's Word of truth and humble their pride to apply His Word obediently, *things happen.*

Don Stephens, founder of Mercy Ships International, has confirmed to me an account of what happened to the group of YWAMers (Youth With A Mission missionaries) who were virtually out of food while the hospital ship *Anastasis* was in dry dock in Athens more than twenty years ago.

Someone had received a cassette tape of my teaching on "Shouting Grace! Grace!" and had played it for the group. Upon hearing the Word of God taught on this subject, and notwithstanding the simple, yet humbling summons to shout, the group prayed together and while praising God began to shout "Grace! Grace!"

What happened the next day defied imagination, and stunned the local community of fishermen in the area. In the morning, the waters around the *Anastasis* began to teem with fish. Suddenly the fish began literally to throw themselves onto the shore. The YWAMers came down the gangway and began to gather the fish—and the phenomenon continued until their freezers were full! And again, Athenians affirmed they had never seen anything like this—an event that not only supplied food miraculously, but also opened the door to a witness for Jesus Christ to those in the area who marveled over what they had seen. The ship's crew testified to them what they had done in claiming God's promise: "Not by might, not by power, but by My Spirit!"

Worship, above all else, is honoring God—who is capable beyond our imagination, loving beyond our deserving, faithful beyond our weakness and gracious beyond our limits. Zerubbabel's Temple was completed to the glory of God. It is a fact of history. Grace works!

Saying "Amen"

Another of the power principles of the Bible is the spiritually discerning use of the word *Amen.* Used with understanding it can be significant in both an individual's and a congregation's life since it is a statement affirming confidence in the dynamic of God's order, His promise and His power.

The Misuse of "Amen"

While it is a biblical principle, the saying of "Amen" has become misused. In some church traditions there are those who take great delight in thundering "Amen!" as a way of announcing that they agree with something being said, whether it is a statement of affirmation or protest; a means of guaranteeing that everyone knows "where I stand." Peculiarly, "Amen" has even been used inappropriately to allow anger in a church service—occurring usually when some worldly unrighteousness is assailed by a preacher and in angered agreement, a self-righteous "Amen!" ricochets from the walls of the building.

Dynamic Application of "Amen"

The word *Amen* is used in the Scriptures more than 175 times. Essentially it means "It is faithful!" or "That's true!" The significance of the word is its derivation from the Hebrew *awman*, which *Strong's Concordance* shows as a primary verb root referring to a thing being "built up, supported or made permanent"; hence the common definition given the word in English—"so be it" or "let it" or "may it be so."

It is among the 25 occurrences of "Amen" in the Old Testament that we find insights for its use on the lips of God's people. There are four primary purposes:

1. to bind oneself to an oath;
2. to affirm leadership;

3. to affirm correction; and
4. to affirm the Word of God.

To Bind Oneself to an Oath

In the books of the Law, Numbers and Deuteronomy, "Amen" is used fourteen times, twelve of which occur in one passage, Deuteronomy 27:15–26. Strangely, this passage relates to curses that will befall people who act in ways detrimental to the community. After each curse was pronounced, the people were required to say, "Amen." In a preceding list of blessings, this response was not called for. The likely reason for this is because we human beings are generally more ready to receive blessings than we are to take responsibility for failures—especially ones that affect others.

For the Israelites, there was the very real danger that those who transgressed the Law would claim ignorance. The declaration of "Amen" was a means of achieving accountability. By saying "Amen," they were binding themselves with an oath and with a curse. God takes no delight in this kind of judgment, but the children of Israel needed to be aware that their disobedience had repercussions both for the community and for themselves.

To Affirm Leadership

In 1 Chronicles 16:36, when the Ark was returned to its rightful place in the heart of God's people, King David read a psalm he wrote to praise God, and then it says, "All the people said, 'Amen!' and praised the LORD." In 1 Kings 1:36, when David has handed over the rulership of the kingdom of Israel to his son Solomon, Benaiah, one of the military leaders, responds, "Amen! May the LORD God of my lord the king say so too." On both these occasions "Amen" is used to affirm leadership. In the first case the people are affirming that the rule of God's Kingdom should be in their midst. In the second case, Benaiah, as the leader of the military, is affirming that he will back the reign of King Solomon.

Through the psalms the people of Israel are taught to say "Amen" as a part of their praise (see Psalms 41, 72, 89, 106). "Amen" is an affirmation of what is transpiring; it affirms that (a) we are together and (b) we support what leadership is calling us to do.

To Affirm Correction

Using his authority as regional governor, Nehemiah steps in to deal with a clear matter of injustice among the people of God. Some of the poor among the returned exiles are coming under severe financial hardship as a result of exploitation of their financial need by their fellow Jews. In response, "All the assembly said, 'Amen!' and praised the LORD" (Nehemiah 5:13). By saying "Amen" they affirm Nehemiah's correction of them.

The same is true in Paul's letters to the young pastor Timothy, in which he uses the affirmation "Amen" five times. There are times when a pastor, as a loving shepherd, needs to correct and guide sheep—members of his flock. On such occasions, it is important that people receive and affirm the correction. Saying "Amen" is not to say, "The pastor is right." It is to say, "The Lord's Word and ways are right," and to submit to that Word by committing to accept it and move toward whatever adjustment is necessary.

(I have found, on the few occasions I have ever done this—and only with leaders, not the congregation—that if I approach my people not with accusation but with the idea that "we [not just "they"] have apparently not seen or understood the matter before," that explanation and application are accepted, including a readiness to move forward with appropriate proposed adjustment to align with God's Word. I have also found it wisest to, in advance, have the elders of the congregation move with me on the matter as we *together* acknowledge our need first, and lead the way in declaring whatever repentance or appropriate adjustment we need to make.)

To Affirm the Word of God

In Nehemiah 8:6, when the scroll of the Law was opened after having not been heard for many years, the people expressed reverence and affirmation for it by saying "Amen":

> And Ezra blessed the LORD, the great God. Then all the people answered, "Amen, Amen!" while lifting up their hands. And they bowed their heads and worshiped the LORD with their faces to the ground.

This "Amen" is essentially saying: What God has established of His Word and will in heaven, we declare, "So shall it be on earth." It leads to the dynamic New Testament practice of Bible believers who, as a part of their worship, honor the eternal Word of God and welcome the promises it contains—in Jesus' name.

Jesus and "Amen"

In the New Testament, the word *Amen* occurs about 150 times. Twenty-four of these times are at the conclusion of a book; only three New Testament books do not end with it. The significance of the word *Amen* at the conclusion of the books of the Bible is simply as a statement of affirmation of the truth they contain and, obviously, its absence at the end of a book does not neutralize our belief in the truth in the book.

The astounding fact about the Bible's use of the word *Amen* is that it occurs most frequently on the lips of Jesus Himself—101 times in the New Testament. *Amen* is the original Greek word, which has been translated as "verily" or "truly." It appears 25 times in John's gospel alone—for example, the classic KJV text, "Verily, verily I say unto you. . . ."

In these cases, by saying "Amen," Jesus is issuing a divine affirmation of the truth of His Word. In essence, He is saying, "Sharpen your hearing and your sensitivities—you are being given eternal Truth and it is being affirmed by My Presence—the Word Incarnate."

He was saying that the Word of the Father, what was and is forever established in heaven, was now becoming applied by God *personally* on earth: "And the *Word* became flesh and dwelt among us, and we beheld His glory, the glory as of the only begotten of the Father, full of grace and truth" (John 1:14, emphasis added).

By saying, "Amen, Amen," Jesus affirms the divinity, authority and the mightiness of the Word of God, and by this we come to the primary point on the subject of "Amen"—that in the Person of Jesus, we have the affirmation of the trustworthiness of all the promises of God: "For all the promises of God in Him are Yes, and in Him Amen, to the glory of God through us" (2 Corinthians 1:20).

All of God's promises channel through one vehicle: the Person of Jesus who calls Himself the "Amen" (see Revelation 3:14). He is the embodiment of God's Word; the affirmation of God's will and purpose on earth. He is "the way, the truth, and the life" (John 14:6). He is "the fullness of the Godhead bodily" (Colossians 2:9) and all that the

Godhead has to say. The Word has been made evident through Him.

All the promises of the Bible—whether in the Old Testament or the New—are affirmed in Jesus. God became flesh and dwelt among us in order that all His promises might be realized in the flesh. He wants us to see in Jesus the personification of His loving desire to make His Word— His life—happen where people are, and in and through whom we each become. He wants to incarnate not only the truth of His Word in us, but the very person of His Son.

The Divine "Amen" of Confirmation

When Jesus came preaching "The Kingdom of heaven is at hand," He was saying that God's will and God's rule are for here and now, and that He was here to affirm it. Today in the living Church, the Lord says, in effect: "If you will hold forth My Word, I will honor it. If you will declare My Word, I will affirm it by the working of my Holy Spirit." In short, He is saying, "If you will declare My Word, I'll say 'Amen!' to it!"

It is the very thing Mark 16:20 says: "And they went out and preached everywhere, the Lord working with them and *confirming the word* through the accompanying signs" (emphasis added). And with that, the book concludes: *"Amen"* (emphasis added).

Some may see it simply as a personal opinion, but I would contend that:

- since Jesus makes so much of "Amen," in the frequency of His using it;
- since no word of God's Word ought to be trivialized by meaningless use;

- since all the promises of God are invested with an "Amen" in Christ Himself; and
- since, finally, Jesus calls Himself "the Amen, the Faithful and True" (Revelation 3:14)...

...*Amen* is no ordinary word to be bandied about either by mere habit or as a specialty shout of a member or two. Neither does it deserve to be intoned passively at the conclusion of prayers during a worship service, as though it were merely noting "The End." Whenever a congregation takes hold of the Word of God, whenever an individual stands upon God's truth and functions in its promise, we make room for the Holy Spirit to move and to actuate the revealed purpose of the Father in His Word.

He who spoke worlds into being, initiating the creative process, is the One who became flesh and dwelt among us. God has not only given us letters on a page, but placed the living Word in our hearts—begotten by the Holy Spirit, that we may speak that Word in the name of that One who is the Word made flesh, the Amen.

"Amen" is the establishing of the living Word of God in the arena of human enterprise and experience for the glory of Jesus Christ. In Jesus is fulfilled the affirmation of God's rule and power, and as we speak "Amen" we invite that rule into our lives, our circumstances and our world.

PART 3

THE PURSUIT OF
WORSHIP

Hail to the Cross

Come with me to Calv'ry's mountain, Come to the Cross.
Come and wash in Calv'ry's fountain, Come to the Cross.
To the place where Christ died for us,
Where He paid the Blood-price for us,
Come and lift this joyous chorus, Come to the Cross.

Praise the Lamb who bled and died there, There at the Cross.
Jesus who was crucified there, There at the Cross.
Through His Blood—that crimson token,
All hell's power has been broken;
"It is finished" has been spoken, There at the Cross.

Here is reason for rejoicing, Here at the Cross.
Grounds for highest praises voicing, Here at the Cross.
Here the sin-curse Jesus severed,
Here He bought us life forever;
Here He'll keep and leave us never, Here at the Cross.

Here is heav'ns eternal treasure: God planned the Cross.
Wealth of love in endless measure, God planned the Cross.
Since His Son has bled and died there,
All my hope for life is tied there;
For God says I'm justified there, God planned the Cross.

Jesus saves and Jesus heals us all through the Cross.
By redemption's pow'r He seals us, All through the Cross.
In the wake of human sinning,
Jesus brought a new beginning;
By His death this promise winning, All through the Cross.

By the Cross we are forgiven, Hail to the Cross.
By the Cross we'll enter heaven, Hail to the Cross.
Through God's love and grace amazing,
We shall join in endless praising;
So this anthem now we're raising, Hail to the Cross.

J.W.H.

CHAPTER 12

Growing a Lifestyle of Worship

The Sacrifice of Worship

Therefore by Him let us continually offer the sacrifice of praise to God, that is, the fruit of our lips, giving thanks to His name.

Hebrews 13:15

The common denominator of the Bible's outstanding people of faith is that they each endured seasons of difficulty and stress, just as you and I do. Every one of us is, at times, vulnerable to the temptation to doubt that we will realize those hopes and purposes Father God has intended for us. Notwithstanding our trust in God's promise that His intent is to give us "a future and a hope" (Jeremiah 29:11), there are occasions when people of genuine faith are challenged by doubt and uncertainty about our own limitations.

Abraham was a man not in any way unlike you or me in this regard. He believed God was faithful, but it is clear—not to mention comforting—that we see times when he became discouraged by the fact that the blessings he clearly understood to be within God's purpose and calling had not yet been fulfilled. Notable in this regard is the exchange between God and Abraham in Genesis 15:1, as the Lord says, "Do not be afraid, Abram. I am your shield, your exceedingly great reward."

Who can but take heart to see Abraham's fear and frustration? He responds by asking God how the circumstances confronting him could be reckoned with the promise made to him. Promised by God that his descendants would be as innumerable as "the dust of the earth" (Genesis 13:16), Abraham's reply is discouraged and downcast: "Lord GOD, what will You give me, seeing I go childless?" (Genesis 15:2). The conversation is brief, but an affirmation and a clearer understanding of the whole picture is coming to Abraham.

The Lord tells him to step outside and *look up*—to see how infinitely greater was His creative power than all of Abraham's notions. The assurance that the promised child will not come by natural means but by a miraculous recapacitation of Abraham's and Sarah's aging bodies. Then—and how pivotal this is—the Lord directs him to *build another altar*. And further, it will be at that altar Abraham will have God's covenant reaffirmed to him.

WHEN YOUR LIFE IS ON THE LINE, LOOK UP

When Abraham stated that he had no heir, the significance is that the future of his family, not to mention his understanding and faith in God's promise, were on the line. Anyone can feel the tension of such a situation. We've all had the question at some time or another: When is God's purpose for my life going to find increase, multiplication, or some assured durability or prospect for the future?

As God brings him outside, a timeless lesson distills for us all—a truth shining from the marvel of creation's splendor surrounding us. He speaks, "Look now toward heaven, and count the stars if you are able to number them.... So shall your descendants be" (Genesis 15:5).

The message is sparklingly clear: The innumerable stars of the sky demonstrated God's endlessly available ability to create. In short, when you feel you've come to the point that fear predicts that your "life" is barricaded against a future, *look up* ... then *build an altar.* Just as there are great lessons when God shows you the stars, there are pointed lessons when you kneel to build an altar in His presence.

THE WAY TO BUILD AN ALTAR

To begin, altars are usually built of broken things.

Ancient altars were built of rock and stone, which prompts reflecting on the geologic process by which they occur. Cracked open under the stress of heat or cold, or the shattered remnants from volcanic explosions or violent shaking, rocks are "hard things" that we encounter—small parts of the larger difficulties comprising a whole planet.

Life has its own "volcanic" upheavals—when relationships overheat and sear, or when the coldness of rejection stings our hearts. Circumstantial seismic events grind over or around us, leaving a trail of brokenness in their path and piling up a wall of doubt before us. What we do then becomes decisive. We can drag disappointment, resentment or hurt around with us, and become burdened with the weight of these stone-like things. Worse, we can retaliate: get mad and throw those things at somebody else.

Or we can do what God told Abraham to do.

We can gather up those hard, broken things and lay them before the Lord—building an altar and worshiping the One who holds our lives and our tomorrows, and who never forgets His promise!

SACRIFICE ALWAYS HAPPENS AT AN ALTAR

The Lord instructed Abraham to sacrifice the lives of three animals and two birds at the altar, an action that is fundamental to all sacrifice: The pouring out of blood represents the pouring out of *life* before God (see Genesis 15:8–10).

Of course, central to this lesson is the picture every Old Testament sacrifice provides of Christ, our Savior. In His death, Jesus perfected the Old Testament sacrificial system— His is the blood that was shed once for all on our behalf—the Lamb of God that takes away the sin of the world (see John 1:29). In Him, we are summoned to pour out our lives in a bloodless sacrifice of worship—to offer our bodies, as well as our minds and spirits, as a *living* sacrifice (see Romans 12:1).

In that light, we capture the New Testament concept: Worshiping God ultimately calls us to the sacrifice of ourselves. Whether it is our "hard" and "broken" things with which we struggle, or the surrender of everything that is summoned by God's call and purpose for our lives— worship calls us to the altar of sacrifice. And once there, we'll find yet another requirement—to see the sacrifice secured.

WATCH OUT FOR VULTURES

After Abraham laid out the sacrificed animals and birds, vultures descended upon the carcasses, and Abraham had to drive them away (see Genesis 15:11). Like the vultures, our adversary or our flesh rebels against full surrender. Every imaginable argument will plead against our "reasonable service"; or circumstances may seem to intrude to steal our resolve. In any case, when such occurs, like Abraham, you and I will need to rise, resist and drive away the vultures.

THE LORD KEEPS HIS PROMISES

We need not fear full yieldedness in pouring ourselves out to the Lord. God promised Abraham that He would be His "shield"—a promise that He makes to us, too.

What the Lord had planned for Abraham was of far greater consequence than merely his becoming the father of a child. After Abraham drove away the vultures from the sacrifice he had made at the altar, the Lord showed him what would happen four centuries ahead to the people he would beget:

> Now when the sun was going down, a deep sleep fell upon Abram; and behold, horror and great darkness fell upon him. Then He said to Abram: "Know certainly that your descendants will be strangers in a land that is not theirs, and will serve them, and they will afflict them four hundred years. And also the nation whom they serve I will judge; afterward they shall come out with great possessions. Now as for you, you shall go to your fathers in peace; you shall be buried at a good old age. But in the fourth generation they shall return here, for the iniquity of the Amorites is not yet complete."
>
> Genesis 15:12–16

The Lord is letting Abraham know that what He plans to do in his life is going to have impact on generations after him. Would the Lord forsake those future generations by forgetting Abraham? We can derive from this that the Lord will keep His promises to us not only because He loves us, but because His future promises depend upon it.

In the midst of Abraham's fear and inability to see beyond the moment, the Bible says that God sent His divine flame to shed light upon the situation—"a smoking oven and a burning torch," and that on that *same day*, the Lord made a covenant with him:

> And it came to pass, when the sun went down and it was dark, that behold, there appeared a smoking oven and a burning torch that passed between those pieces. On the same day the LORD made a covenant with Abram, saying: "To your descendants I have given this land, from the river of Egypt to the great river, the River Euphrates."
>
> Genesis 15:17–18

However uncertain tomorrow seems, in this lesson from Abraham's life, we can hear the Lord saying to us: "To build altars of worship and surrender, pour out yourself, your fears, your doubts, your frustrations as 'living sacrifices.'" As we do, God will bring light into our darkness, renew the confidence of His covenant with us, and assure us that His promise has not been forgotten and is certain to be fulfilled.

PEOPLE OF FAITH OFFER THE SACRIFICE OF WORSHIP

Beyond every Old Testament picture, the New Testament calls us to the timeless assurance of the covenant we have with God through the ultimate altar of Calvary and the final sacrifice made in the Person of Jesus (see Hebrews 13:10–15). The glory of this reality calls us more than to the solution of our doubts and fears, but to the establishing of a lifestyle of worship: "Therefore by Him let us continually offer the sacrifice of praise to God, that is, the fruit of our lips, giving thanks to His name"—to the building of a "house of worship" framed where we live.

The blueprint and materials for such a construction can be found in the rich legacy of the book of Psalms, as God's unchanging truths regarding worship overflow from its pages. David's exhortations calling ancient Israel to praise and worship the Lord were the same guidelines applied as New Testament believers began to learn to worship. The principles are timeless, and the call to a Davidic order of humility, confession and repentance, childlikeness and heart-openness before the Lord are instructive for building either a congregation's or an individual's worship life.

BUILDING A HOUSE OF WORSHIP WHERE YOU LIVE

"Present your bodies a living sacrifice"—the apostle Paul's call to worship (Romans 12:1)—calls us to begin with a very practical, personal, forthright style of private worship; to make *your* home a worship center. Whatever your domestic status—whether you have a believing spouse or family, live alone or are a single parent—the key element is in your own personal response to God's call.

This is no call to construct a shrine or to shape a private chapel structure. The "building" is the presentation of our body, or voice, our heart and our full personal availability to God, His presence and His Word. Here are some pointers:

- **Kneel.** *"Oh come, let us worship and bow down; let us kneel before the LORD our Maker"* (Psalm 95:6). Kneeling is an acknowledgment of submission; a way to bring anything under Christ's dominion. I have cultivated a habit of kneeling in worship to the Lord as I get out of bed each morning, affirming that He is the ruler of my household, my life and my family. Making a "Sonrise" declaration of Jesus Christ invites and welcomes His presence into my day.

- **Sing.** *"Oh come, let us sing to the LORD! Let us shout joyfully to the Rock of our salvation"* (Psalm 95:1). Singing worship to the Lord releases joy. It refreshes and renews us even in times of pain, and it helps us maintain a fresh flow of the Spirit of the Lord in and through our lives. Whatever the quality of your voice, you will be blessed when you sing the praises of God during both abundant and wilderness seasons.

- **Invite God to dinner.** *"My mouth shall speak the praise of the LORD"* (Psalm 145:21). Where a family is in harmony of faith in the Lord, this can be a beautiful part of your table talk. Don't create an atmosphere of forced or pompous piety, but look for pleasant—even fun—points of teaching and ministry to your children, allowing each person to have a part, sharing points of praise over "what Jesus is doing in my life."

- **Pray . . . while feeding on the Word.** *"For where two or three are gathered together in My name, I am there in the midst of them"* (Matthew 18:20). Along with private devotions, pray together with your spouse, family or others in your household, inviting everyone to share prayer requests. Make it a time of openness and liberty. Occasionally speak the creative Word of God aloud in your home.

- **Worship in your spiritual language.** *"I will pray with the spirit, and I will also pray with the understanding. I will sing with the spirit, and I will also sing with the understanding"* (1 Corinthians 14:15). Our praise abounds beyond all human limitation when we worship the Lord, both with our best understanding as we declare His goodnesses, and with the broadened capacity the Holy Spirit gives our speech when we exhaust its possibilities, saying with Charles Wesley, "O for a thousand tongues to sing [or speak] my great Redeemer's praise!"

- **Have Communion.** *"Do this in remembrance of Me"* (1 Corinthians 11:24; see verses 24–26). When we celebrate Communion, we are celebrating the grandest altar of all—the cross of Calvary upon which the Son of God was laid as the sacrifice to reconcile all humankind to God. It is perfectly biblical and proper to let your home be a place where the testimony of what Jesus accomplished in His death and resurrection is lifted up in this way. This, of course, is not to substitute for corporate worship with a congregation, but is to declare the covenant of Calvary in your home as well.

PEOPLE OF FAITH ARE PEOPLE WHO WORSHIP

Never make the mistake of supposing that a person of faith is someone who has found the master key of life and that everything that person touches turns to gold. That is not what constitutes the evidence of a person of faith. There isn't anybody like that in the world. What makes people of faith is what they do in the face of trials: When their lives are on the line, people of faith worship. Abraham is called the "father of the faithful" because at every encounter, he brought his hard things, laid them before the Lord and offered the sacrifice of worship. His pathway of altars and worship marks a trail for those of us who seek to become people of faith.

When your life is on the line, focus on worship and *look up*; take your eyes off your circumstances and onto Him. Come to Jesus in the same way Abraham came to an altar— bewildered, frustrated, stumbling, in doubt and yet still believing. Build an altar of your broken things; pour yourself out and worship God there; and then listen to Him talk to you in the middle of that situation.

In response, He bestows His glory upon you when you worship—returning in blessing what you have offered in praiseful worship, as the psalmist so triumphantly declares:

> You have turned for me my mourning into dancing;
> You have put off my sackcloth and clothed me with
>   gladness,
> To the end that my glory may sing praise to You and not
>   be silent.
> O LORD my God, I will give thanks to You forever.
>
> Psalm 30:11–12

CHAPTER 13

Furnishing the Tabernacle

The Pattern for Worship

How lovely is Your tabernacle,
O LORD of hosts!

Psalm 84:1

Over the past eight years I have met with a contingent of 35–45 different pastors for one full week each month. The broad range of pastoral challenges and ministry issues we cover includes, as anyone would suppose, a component on "the worshiping congregation." In that portion of my interaction with these seasoned leaders—many having been in ministry more than twenty years, I am always surprised at the response I receive when I inquire, "What happened at Mount Sinai?"

This question is usually preceded by a half-hour long presentation I make on God's call to Moses, to "bring the people that they may worship [serve] Me on this mountain" (see Exodus 3:12). Having elaborated on Moses' miraculous encounter with God at the burning bush, and God's subsequent outlining of His intention to deliver Israel from slavery and bring them into His gracious and abounding purposes for them, the call to worship at Sinai becomes most remarkable. God was essentially saying, "The way to realize My purposes is to learn to worship!" All the more remarkable is it in the light of 1 Corinthians 10 which specifically notes that Israel's experiences at this time in her history were for the New Testament Church believers' learning and application. That is, to say it again, "The way to realize God's purposes in our life is to learn to worship!"

That's the point where I ask the question: "What happened at Sinai?"

The first answers are always predictable: "God gave the Ten Commandments." "The golden calf episode occurred." "The tablets were broken and a new set of the Commandments were needed." And the beat goes on.... And among the thousands of good, biblically-centered leaders who have joined me at the JWH School of Pastoral Nurture, only *one* has, with virtual immediacy, mentioned the building of the Tabernacle!

WORSHIP AND THE WORD

Whether mention finally comes from a participant in the class or on my own part, finally saying it myself, I draw a simple diagram on the board:

| The Tablets | The Word | The Law |
| The Tabernacle | Their Worship | The Liturgy |

The details God gave Moses for Israel's worship have, for the most part, been exceeded or fulfilled today. Christ, in His life as the sinless Lamb, in His death as the sacrificial substitute, in His ministry as our Great High Priest—in His beauty and perfection as the Fulfiller of all things Holy—has *completed* the redemptive work that now affords a fellowship with God for every repentant sinner. Hallelujah!!

Still, the Bible—notably, throughout the book of Hebrews —makes very clear that lessons in worship still await the one who comes to the Tabernacle to see its magnificent, predictive "photographs" of Christ and of our worship. God's Word—the Center Piece in our worship, holds forth picture upon picture of our relationship with and worship of Jesus here—the Central Person in our worship. And that fact establishes a full legitimacy for our studying the furnishings of the Tabernacle; looking into the unfolding beauty of Jesus Christ as each object employed in worship draws us to love and praise Him more. Thus, here on this mountain, where God would first deliver His Word, we are being led to balance *worship and the Word* in our life—both personally and as a congregation. Here, as worship is unfolded to the Israelites and they are instructed in its purity and power, God is teaching them how to walk in His ways. Not only would they begin to learn how to live as people of promise—as free men and women—but they will also shortly learn that both *their destiny* and *His objective* could only thus be fully realized.

"Now therefore, if you will indeed obey My voice and keep My covenant, then you shall be a special treasure to Me

above all people; for all the earth is Mine. And you shall be
to Me a kingdom of priests and a holy nation."

Exodus 19:5 6

Paramount to fulfillment of God's objective was their
obedience to His Word and right relationship to His ways.
Like the children of Israel, you and I as former slaves now
liberated from sin's bondage and captivity by Jesus Christ
our Savior, are welcomed to learn the priestly ministry of
worship as a pathway of growth and deepening purpose
(see 1 Peter 2–3). It is this ministry—worship—that begets
the environment in which we grow to partner in God's
Kingdom rule and ministry to the world around us. Thus,
our destiny as redeemed slaves is gloriously declared by the
angels, elders and living creatures—a passage that calls us to
worship with the understanding that thereby we, as mere
humans, are restored to a place of functional partnership
with almighty God in administrating life-issues in the
everyday world we live in.

"For You were slain,
And have redeemed us to God by Your blood
Out of every tribe and tongue and people and nation,
And have made us kings and priests to our God;
And we shall reign on the earth."

Revelation 5:9–10

And just as there is a *purpose* to our worship—the entry of
God's glory and the restoration of our reigning partnership
with Him on earth—so there is also a *pattern*. At Mount Sinai,
the Lord provided explicit specifications to the Israelites
about how to build the place where, at the invitation of
their worship, He would meet with them—the Tabernacle.
Four times in the preparation for building the Tabernacle, the Lord stressed that it be built according to a pattern:

> Then the LORD spoke to Moses, saying: "Speak to the children of Israel.... And let them make Me a sanctuary, that I may dwell among them. According to all that I show you, that is, the pattern of the tabernacle and the pattern of all its furnishings, just so shall you make it."
>
> Exodus 25:1, 8–9

In every article and furnishing of the Tabernacle, there is a lesson to be learned and a picture of Jesus to be seen.

THE TABERNACLE

The Tabernacle of Israel's time was a moveable tent—a temporary dwelling place in the wilderness. In fact, the word *tabernacle* means "tent." The people of Israel were constantly on the move, and they needed a structure that could travel with them. The lesson to former slaves who were learning to walk with God was that through their worship, they could invite God's glory into their midst.

In the Person of His Son, Jesus, God became flesh and "tabernacled" among us. For His redeemed "nation of priests," the tabernacle is no longer contained within a building or a tent—the Lord wants to meet us and to dwell with each of us wherever we are: "Behold, the tabernacle of God is with men, and He will dwell with them, and they shall be His people. God Himself will be with them and be their God" (Revelation 21:3).

THE BRAZEN ALTAR

The brazen or brass altar near the entrance to the Tabernacle was where the sacrifice took place. The worshiper brought an animal to be sacrificed, which represented payment for his own sin. God accepted a substitute sacrifice in order that the worshiper's sins could be forgiven and he could continue to live and worship Him.

Offering the sacrifice was a deeply personal experience. Placing his hand on the animal's head, the worshiper would acknowledge that the animal was being killed in his place. Its shed blood would be caught in a basin, and on the Day of Atonement, or Yom Kippur, the high priest would take the blood into the "holy of holies," a sacred room separated from the main Tabernacle by a veil. Only the high priest was allowed to enter the Holy Place; a classic depiction of the fact that only as we identify with Christ—God's ultimate, conclusive sacrifice—may we enter into God's presence (see John 14:6).

The Laver

The laver was a giant basin in which everyone on the pathway to worship would wash in order to be purified. Purification acknowledged that worship not only calls for a substitutionary sacrifice. Just as in Moses' time He called His worshipers to wash at the laver, so we are summoned to seek His presence in worship, and as we do, the Lord points the way to a cleansing release, not only from the guilt of sin but from its residue, delivered from its incrustation in our lives, and released from all that taints the memory and induces relentless guilt or shame into the human psyche. Just as we are called to come, we are given a promise: "If we confess our sins, He is faithful and just to forgive us our sins and to cleanse us from all unrighteousness" (1 John 1:9). We are assured we can be cleansed from past shame:

For if the blood of bulls and goats and the ashes of a heifer, sprinkling the unclean, sanctifies for the purifying of the flesh, how much more shall the blood of Christ, who through the eternal Spirit offered Himself without spot to God, cleanse your conscience from dead works to serve the living God?

Hebrews 9:13–14

The ancient ritual washing with "the ashes of a heifer" was one of the God-ordained pictures given to us, to say that—just as cleansing was afforded at the laver—there is a cleansing today, answering to the plaguing stains of sin remembered though forgiven.

THE TABLE FOR THE SHEWBREAD AND THE LAMPSTAND

Once inside the Tabernacle, the worshiper came to a table where two loaves of bread called the shewbread were arranged. This bread was eaten by the priest who understood that in doing so, he was feeding on more than the bread itself. The mystery of our human need for spiritual nutrition was being taught: "Man shall not live by bread alone; but man lives by every word that proceeds from the mouth of the LORD" (Deuteronomy 8:3).

Further, the shewbread represents the Word of God. Jesus, who is the Word that "became flesh and dwelt among us" (John 1:14), went ever further. He referred to Himself as the "bread of life" (John 6:35), and introduced His own body as the "living bread," which alone can save as well as satisfy. In building a life of worship, the progression of worship depicted in these Tabernacle furnishings deserves to be learned and applied: coming in praise of God for the sacrifice made on our behalf; asking the Lord to purify our lives; then opening and feeding on the Word of God—in spirit and in truth.

Next to the table on which the shewbread was placed was a lampstand—a timelessly beautiful picture of the illumination the Holy Spirit brings to us by the Word and by His voice. The psalmist declares the Spirit's word to us in *precept* (the Scriptures): "Your word is a lamp to my feet and a light to my path" (Psalm 119:105). The prophet Isaiah matches to this the Spirit's word to us *in promptings* (His corrective voice): "Your ears shall hear a word behind you, saying, 'This is the way, walk in it,' whenever you turn [aside] to the right hand . . . or whenever you turn to the left" (Isaiah 30:21). In this way we honor the Savior's desire to not only feed us by His Word, nourishing our understanding, but also to obey His Holy Spirit's inner voice, urging us to make God's Word a *light* to our lives ("a lamp to my feet") and guidance to our walk with Him ("a light to my path").

THE ALTAR OF INCENSE

A special incense, prepared according to specific instructions given by the Lord, was burned on this altar. It had a beautiful, sweet aroma and was not to be used for any purpose other than worshiping the Lord.

Of the New Testament believer, it is beautifully adapted to practical living and Spirit-filled worship:

- *By our witness and faithful constancy before the world*: "For we are to God the fragrance of Christ among those who are being saved and among those who are perishing. To the one we are the aroma of death leading to

death, and to the other the aroma of life leading to life"
(2 Corinthians 2:15–16);

- *By our faithful giving and support to the ministry of the Gospel*: Paul expresses his thanks to the Philippian congregation for their financial support, saying, "The things sent from you (are) a sweet-smelling aroma, an acceptable sacrifice, well pleasing to God" (Philippians 4:18).

- *By our life of prayer and intercession before God*, a worthy sacrifice of worship comes before His throne conjoined to a cloud of incense—even in our day: "Then another angel, having a golden censer, came and stood at the altar. He was given much incense, that he should offer it with the prayers of all the saints . . . before God" (Revelation 8:3, 4).

- *By a poignant illustration of worship's sacrifice* offered by Mary, Lazarus's and Martha's sister. Jesus commends her sacrifice as the fragrance of an expensive perfume fills the house, suggesting the way a New Testament priestly ministry of worship may penetrate the invisible, as the aroma—in this case, not of earthly mixture but heavenly—is wafted into His presence from the hearts of humble souls who present themselves a sacrifice to God (see John 12:3).

The altar of incense points to that beautiful devotion God seeks—a treasure of love and adoration reserved for Himself and Himself alone. His desire to bring us back to Himself through Christ is manifested in even greater depth as His summons to worship calls us to the tender intimacy of deep devotion—discovered in the place where we present our whole being wholeheartedly and unreservedly to Him.

THE VEIL

The veil separated the holy of holies—the most sacred room in the Tabernacle—from the rest of worship area. No one could go past the veil except the high priest who was allowed to enter this revered place once a year on Yom Kippur to offer a blood sacrifice.

This aspect of worship changed when the spear pierced Jesus' side while He hung on the cross, causing blood and water to gush forth. It was at that moment that the last blood sacrifice was accomplished on our behalf. The Bible says that when Jesus breathed His last breath and yielded up His spirit "the veil of the temple was torn in two from top to bottom"; not torn by human hands but by God Himself (Matthew 27:50–51).

In doing so, Father God made His own heaven-executed declaration that He had opened the way into the holy of holies. By reason of Jesus' work and words—"It is finished" —we have these promises:

- "We have a great High Priest who has passed through the heavens, Jesus the Son of God!" (Hebrews 4:14).
- "We do not have a High Priest who cannot sympathize with our weaknesses . . . [so] let us therefore come boldly to the throne of grace, that we may obtain mercy and find grace to help in time of need" (Hebrews 4:15–16).
- "This hope [of God's promised salvation] we have as an anchor of the soul, both sure and steadfast, and which enters the Presence behind the veil, where the forerunner has entered for us, even Jesus, having become High Priest forever . . ." (Hebrews 6:19–20).

THE ARK OF THE COVENANT

The Ark was a box kept in the holiest part of the Tabernacle. Each of the objects contained in the Ark was there for a reason, pointing to an attribute of God's covenant with His people and foreshadowing our relationship with Him through Jesus Christ. In particular, the Ark represents the relationship God seeks with His people through our worship and His Word.

The writer of Hebrews (see 9:1–5) summarizes for us what those contents were: the tablets of stone on which the Ten Commandments were written, representing God's covenant (see Exodus 20; Deuteronomy 5); a golden pot containing a portion of manna—His provision in the wilderness (see Exodus 16); and the rod of Aaron that had budded, signifying his priestly leadership (see Numbers 17).

Although the Ark was the focal point of Israel's worship, neither the Ark itself nor its contents were worshiped; rather, where the Ark was, the Lord displayed His glory in a visible and shining presence. The contents of the Ark represent a picture of our own personal potential within God's promise to those who worship Him; a promise of:

- daily provision, just as the manna was preserved in the Ark for a testimony; and
- a life-flow of grace, just as the miraculously budding rod testifies of the practical, daily-life application of resurrection power toward us (see Ephesians 1:18–20).

THE MERCY SEAT

The lid of the Ark was called the mercy seat. God announced it as the specific place where He would meet people with forgiveness. On the Day of Atonement, the priest would enter the holy of holies and pour a sacrifice of blood on the mercy seat—that is, overflowingly above the stone tablets of God's commandments that were inside—commandments impossible for fallen souls to keep.

Thus, the mercy seat still stands as a testimony, pointing us to the New Testament where Jesus Himself becomes the "Mercy Seat" (Greek *hilasterion*—"that which propitiates, atones, the place of propitiation, the mercy seat" (see Romans 3:25; Hebrews 9:5).

Without the sacrifice of blood, no atonement was worthy (see Leviticus 17:11). The blood of animals, which only *forecast* the redemption to come was inadequate, but the blood of Christ *fulfilled* redemption's price and requirements and has perfected eternal salvation forever for all who come to Him (see Hebrews 9:11–15).

In the picture of the Ark and the mercy seat, God shows us that He does not meet us on our terms or our efforts at fulfilling the *Law*, but on the terms of what Jesus bequeaths us through *grace*—grace made possible by the sacrifice of blood (see Ephesians 2:7–8). By receiving us through His grace at the mercy seat, God is saying, in effect: "I will receive you where you are, but I haven't changed My mind about where I want to take you." So the gravity of God's Word is not to be lost because we receive mercy at the point of our inadequacies, but the glory of the mercy seat announces the hope that He will not only save us from our sin, but also lift us into the glory of His fulfilling purpose in our lives as we walk with Him in worship.

BECOME A TABERNACLE OF WORSHIP!

Right where you are, Christ's salvation has laid the foundation for a temple—for a tabernacle of worship. He invites you to open your life to become a *holy site*—a place where He can meet with you, dwell with you and manifest His presence to you and through you. It is Jesus who makes this possible—"Christ in you, the hope of glory" (Colossians 1:27). So begin to furnish *your* house—the temple of your own being. Build a life of worship, "according to the pattern which was shown you on the mount" (Exodus 25:40). Let each furnishing become a steppingstone to a full-house life of worship, responding to His call that we:

- rejoice in the completed sacrifice Jesus has achieved for us;
- be purified from the things that would clutter or pollute our lives;
- feed on His Word, letting the Holy Spirit illuminate and apply it to our lives;
- lift the sweet fragrance of praise and worship from our hearts to the Lord; and,
- come to the mercy seat, where grace and forgiveness are ever assured . . .

. . . and abide there.

CHAPTER 14

Our Reasonable Service

The Physical Expressions of Worship

My heart and my flesh cry out for the living God.

Psalm 84:2

The service wasn't ten minutes old when the prompting came to my mind—it was more than an impression; it was a clear, concise command spoken to me by the Lord: *Kneel before Me.* It would have been so easy to do in most any setting, but what followed in the next few minutes was a wrestling match—struggling mostly with, *What will people think?*

The location was on the platform of a thriving church in Oregon. The situation was simple: I was the pulpit guest of a friend of mine from college days, in a church of another denomination, and among people who—for the

196

most part—didn't know me. Further, we were seated in pulpit chairs on the platform, facing the congregation— about 400 people—and there was no place to hide. Thus, what seems like a simple assignment was made complex by a dozen thoughts racing through my mind—not thoughts resistant to the idea of kneeling before the Savior, but resistant to kneeling right then and there.

I thought, *I am a visitor. Will people think I am trying to impress them? Or I could be distracting. None of them knows me; they won't even know why I am doing this. They'll think it's some kind of ritual that I do. They'll think I'm trying to "start something."* And as reasons accumulated, a Voice louder than reason was speaking to my mind; Jesus was summoning my heart.

As the worship leader continued leading the people, I sang with sincerity while at the same time wrestling within. Finally, about halfway through the third song, I surrendered—believing the possibility of my own embarrassment preferable to the possibility of disappointing my Lord, or worse, securing a surrender to my pride.

I have long known that God is not going to cast out someone who succumbs to self rather than surrendering to pride or fear's death in such moments. In other words, the issue wasn't, "Do this, or you're going to hell!" But I am equally sure that a life in following Christ is not just one that avoids the highway to eternal perdition; it's also about a life increasing in heaven's *present* reward—the blessing of living with the presence of God and the beauty of His glory in my life.

Remembering that evening's encounter with the Lord and myself, and the struggle between whom to obey, I always find it amusing to remember the most amazing thing I experienced. It was when, after kneeling and worshiping for about a minute or two, I rose and was seated again, only to discover as I opened my eyes that not one person in that congregation had even noticed me. *Not one.* Because as they had been singing, their eyes had all been closed—caught up in worshiping the Lord.

WORSHIP'S FUNDAMENTAL OFFERING

What had attempted to wedge itself into the open flow of worship between me and God was human pride. It's an ever-present threat to full-hearted worship. Since Cain was angered over God's acceptance of that prescribed sacrifice He expected, and his own self-evolved presentation was rejected, choosing to worship "God's way or my way" has been an eventual life-or-death issue. We choose between the living sacrifice of Holy Spirit-filled, biblically described approaches to worship, or the lifeless, non-multiplying habits dictated by human wisdom.

The very definition of the word *worship* is to lay one's self before the Lord. The Greek word for worship, *proskuneo*, means to prostrate oneself before God, to lay one's face to the ground, humbled before Him. It is not a stance of groveling to gain divine favor, but rather one that acknowledges the weight and worthiness of His glory.

To literally do that in a large public assembly, as I felt called to do that night, would neither be required nor even practical in most situations. But consider: Even in the privacy of your own home, have you ever—would you readily be willing to prostrate yourself before God? Such a self-confrontation, challenging our oft-insistent preoccupation with our self-consciousness *even when no one else is present*, faces us with a subject worth exploring.

Paul's call to worship, "Present your bodies a living sacrifice," not only indicates this is our reasonable, spiritual, logically appropriate and righteous choice, but adds: "... and do not be conformed to this world, but be transformed by the renewing of your mind..." (Romans 12:2). The focus turns to the "will of God," and demonstrates the direct relationship between worship—the essence of submission to God—and a life that moves forward into full effectiveness in line with one's God and Creator.

A CHOICE FOR CHILDLIKE WORSHIP

David, the Bible's greatest instructor in worship—given his writing in Psalms—is also one of the Bible's greatest warriors, greatest kings and greatest men by any measure. He was neither a coward nor a wimp, nor an idiot, fanatic or unreasoning person. And this makes his model of humility all the more instructive as we consider worship's call to "present ourselves"—*all* of ourselves.

Second Samuel 6 records a highly instructive occasion—one that includes King David's dancing openly in joyful, unabashed worship before the Lord.

At this time, Jerusalem had come under David's control, and he was bent toward establishing his capital as a center of worship to the Living God. His own personal intimacy with God, joined to his awareness that worship is the fountainhead of all fruitfulness—leadership, management, governance, economics and so forth—prompted his passion. The complete story of the retrieval of the Ark of the Covenant from the downward spiral of its travels and capture from Israel during the season of Saul's spiritual attrition is contained in the adjacent passages. But it is in chapter 6 that David seeks to bring the Ark back among God's people. There are several lessons inherent in the unwitting miscalculation David makes in his first attempt. But having received the counsel of the priests of Israel, and adjusted his approach to the Ark's transportation, this colossal symbol of God's presence among His people is now being ushered into the city where Yahweh has said, "I will put My name there." Overjoyed, and simultaneously humbled at God's pleasure with his purpose to bring home the Ark, David "danced before the LORD with all his might" (verse 14). The episode is highly relevant to our thoughts about the worship of God.

The lesson we would wisely draw is not a mandate to follow his model in every service we experience, or for every day in our lives. But there is a message—a study in contrasts—between two kinds of people: those who are neither preoccupied with their own dignity nor bound to their own pride, and those who are gripped by both and gripped by people who are otherwise.

The whole passage is worth a reverent reading. Michal, David's wife and the daughter of Saul, is the picture of self-preservation and what that produces—ultimate defeat. Watching David "leaping and whirling before the LORD" from her window, Michal "despised him in her heart" (verse 16), and she confronts and assails her husband for his dance (see verse 20). The lesson should never be carried over to the point that it becomes an argument for the individualized, self-centeredness of idiosyncratic worshipers "doing their own thing" in church, but ought to be wisely examined as a warning against "preserving my own flesh" in church, or anywhere else. Michal's life-long childlessness (doubtless because David refused to ever engage her in lovemaking again) depicts the emptiness of worship that surrenders to fleshly wisdom and pride rather than the simplicity of worship with humility. At the same time, we are given a lesson in the direct relationship between worship and fruitfulness. Life flows where people are willing to humble themselves, and to walk and worship joyfully and transparently before the Savior who has so magnificently shown His grace to us.

OBSTACLES TO WORSHIP

There are at least three obstacles that we face when we begin to worship: (1) the ecclesiastical, (2) the political or social and (3) the personal and subjective within ourselves.

The Ecclesiastical Obstacle

Just as there can be an unseemly fanaticism of ludicrous display, there is also a ready and equal fanaticism of silence and reserve that can preoccupy people. Perhaps this is a result of thought patterns evolving in eras of Church history into a great divorce between the spiritual and the physical that shapes us to this day. In the monastic era, for example, spirituality was sought by removing oneself as far as possible from the physical realities of the outside world. Silence, separation and celibacy were seen as signs of holiness. At other times, including today, intellectualism tends to argue the same dichotomy—the spiritual (or mental) is deemed superior to the physical, and worship becomes thereby "intellectualized." Thus, reserve and silence often hang like a cloud over congregations, having been licensed to press against or hinder heartfelt, liberated, biblically expressive worship breaking out of tradition's box. Fear that letting go—and of "anything goes" taking over—leads to licensing a suppression of the simplest and loveliest expressions of sensible, sensitive and scripturally invited worship.

Honesty in the light of history's imposed habits requires us to look into the Book. Time after time in the Psalms, strong Hebrew verbs are used in connection with praising the Lord, making it clear that the Lord is calling for the open expression of His people. Still, for example, we have sometimes sanctified silence, making it define "reverence." Even though there is a time for silence, the two words are not synonyms. Ecclesiastes 3:7 says there is "a time to keep silence, and a time to speak." Psalm 46:10 says, "Be still and know that I am God." But with an equal, if not even broader summons, the Word of God calls us to shout and to sing the high praises of our God—to so acknowledge the grace of God and the triumph of His Son's cross that we're told, "Clap your hands...Shout to God" (Psalm 47:1). Both silence and a shout, quietness or high praise can express reverence, but if reserve and stillness are defined as "reverence," then the full-orbed reverence of liberated worship will suffer limitations. Even more danger-ous, the insistence of human pride and posturing will be granted freedom to dominate.

The Socio-Political Obstacle

In my own nation, the culture of our politics has strangely played into the idea that "I can decide how to worship God on my own." To what degree this exists in other nations, I am not qualified to say, but while we are assured of the legal and moral right to worship God "according to the dictates of our hearts" (a precious liberty), there is nothing in the

Bible that says we can approach God in worship on our own terms—ever.

The truth is, once any one of us chooses to worship the Living God, who gave His Son, Jesus Christ, to die for us on the cross, we technically remove ourselves from the realm of selective privilege as to *how* we will worship Him. No longer is worship according to "the dictates of my own heart." More specifically, if I'm interested in discovering the full release of grace, power and blessing of God's manifest presence, I am called from my ideas to God's Word. To examine the Bible on the subject of worship is to be moved into the realm of spirit and truth—to the worship summoned by the Holy Spirit and summarized in the Word of Truth—the truth that God has revealed in His Word.

As we saw in our study on furnishing the Tabernacle, God gave Moses explicit instructions about how His people were to worship. We know that when a builder is constructing a building, an early mistake can be disabling—may even result in the whole structure having to be dismantled in order to avoid disaster. Thus, the question that faces each of us personally—and church leaders realistically—is, How much dismantling might be needed in my/our thinking regarding worship's expressions?

This is not an issue of whether we are saved or not. To be saved, it is obviously not a requirement that we, for example, lift our arms, clap hands, shout aloud or even sing! Salvation—experiencing God's love and mercies—is rooted and grounded in one thing: faith in Jesus Christ alone as God's Son, humanity's only Savior and the worthy Lamb of God.

But the thrust of this book is one born of a burden—a passion and desire to experience the *manifest presence of God*—the release of His Kingdom grace and Kingdom power, moving among and abiding amidst His people. It's a pursuit that calls us to honesty about confronting our human pride, diagnosing and casting down the fear that can hinder us, as well as refusing the folly of fanaticism that will always seek to interpose itself when living, revitalized, biblical worship opens to the fullest dynamism of God's presence in the Church.

WORSHIP: THE TOTAL BEING MADE ALIVE

Becoming the kind of worshipers that Father God is looking for—those who worship Him "in spirit and truth" (John 4:24)—means that our worship will be called beyond *both* cerebral preoccupation and merely emotional exaggerations. It will call us to come with hearts engaged; empty ritual overthrown as our forms and formats, our liturgies and our lives become enflamed with the fire of God descending upon living sacrifices presenting an acceptable sacrifice to the Lord.

We will discover the full blend of our entire human person and being called before Him, enriched in His presence and transformed by our worship of God. Full-orbed worship, then, is not *just* spiritual and from the heart; neither is it *just* a cerebral pursuit, a mystical consciousness or an emotional binge. But in the light of God's Word, worship is about the presentation of our *total being*—that is, body, mind, emotions and spirit—ignited by the Holy Spirit as a living sacrifice. It is that worship which His Word declares is nothing more than our reasonable service:

> I beseech you therefore, brethren, by the mercies of God, that you present your bodies a living sacrifice, holy, acceptable to God, which is your reasonable service. And do not be

conformed to this world, but be transformed by the renewing of your mind, that you may prove what is that good and acceptable and perfect will of God.

Romans 12:1–2

This New Testament counterpart to Old Testament sacrifice—a text we have examined in its basic implications—opens to a rich application joined to the Bible's many and varied expressions of worship. The Greek word *logikos*, translated "reasonable service" (NKJV) conveys two ideas: both *intelligence* and *spiritual* worship. While in the same verse, Paul's "I beseech you," carries an emotional appeal to ignite similarly sensitive emotionality "therefore," i.e., in the light of all that has preceded in his paean of praise to God in the several verses prior. These—intellect, emotion and spirit—join to "your bodies," to frame a fourfold appeal to we who would worship. With this wholeness of approach, let us come to the altar of God, laying our lives before Him. Let us come humbly, knowing that "the sacrifices of God are a broken spirit, a broken and a contrite heart," of which the Word declares, "these, O God, You will not despise" (Psalm 51:17).

While salvation's offer invites us in the brokenness of our lost estate unto forgiveness and restoration, worship's invitation invites us to wholeness at every dimension as our total being opens in His presence. But just as sinful pride can keep us as sinners from the first, so self-centered pride is able to keep us from the second. And it is exactly that quest—seeing worshipers brought into wholeness as persons—that has moved me to seek ways and wisdom for helping believers to grow in full-spectrumed worship. Teaching the Word of God, and thoughtfully showing how sensitive, gracious and beauty-filled worship may be expressed in song and physical expressions without becoming distracting, disruptive or legalistic, the following has been a helpful guide.

God invites us to worship Him "in spirit and in truth," and "in the beauty of holiness," with our full persons: (1) with our regenerated spirits; (2) with our renewed minds; (3) with our revived emotions; and (4) with our rededicated bodies.

With Regenerated Spirits

"For God is my witness, whom I serve with my spirit in the gospel of His Son" (Romans 1:9). The word *serve* conveys the concept of worship as well as works, specifically noting the power of the new birth to resurrect the human spirit to an aliveness toward God.

- Worshiping in Spirit (John 4:23–24)
- Singing spiritual songs (Ephesians 5:19; Colossians 3:16)
- Giving thanks "well" by the Spirit (1 Corinthians 14:15–17)

As we have noted earlier, "spiritual songs," are those generated by the Holy Spirit as worshipers sing before the Lord. We are also shown how the Holy Spirit will enable us to worship "well," igniting our singing with a holy vitality that converts it from mere melody to a holy incense—from mere sound to heavenly zephyrs of praise.

With Renewed Minds

"But be transformed by the renewal of your mind" (Romans 12:2). Not only does worship require a prerequisite "change of mind" as repentance brings us back to

God through Christ, but worship opens the doorway to a progressive reconditioning of the mind, as we are "transformed ... from glory to glory ... by the Spirit of the Lord" (2 Corinthians 3:18).

Worship is not only intended to proceed from an intellect enlightened *by* the Gospel, but to deepen as the penetration of God's Word reprioritizes our thought processes to glorify Him—the Giver of intelligence—rather than to be captivated by our own brainpower. The human mind, submitted to His Spirit, will learn the true wisdom that accrues only when human intellect ceases to reign as king, and aligns with God's Spirit as He places *spirit* above *reason*. God will never demean our intelligence: He created it and its potential. But by His Spirit ruling in our reborn spirit, He will regularly call us to transcend reason—to exercise faith which, while not unreasonable, regularly exceeds human powers of thought or computation. Thus, worship moves us deeper into the pathways of faith not by employing the highest and best of our thinking, but by bringing it beyond those limits to the richest and fullest of our potential as spiritual-rational beings. We are called to:

- obedient, intelligent worship (Romans 12:1; 2 Corinthians 10:5);
- praying with the understanding (1 Corinthians 14:15); and
- praising with the understanding (Psalm 47:6–7).

With Revived Emotions

"And whatever you do, do it heartily, as to the Lord and not to men" (Colossians 3:23). "Be kindly affectionate to one another with brotherly love ... fervent in spirit, serving the

Lord.... Rejoice with those who rejoice, and weep with those who weep" (Romans 12:10–11, 15).

There is nothing about human emotions that ought to be deemed untrustworthy simply because of their basic essence. Our emotions are God-given as surely as our minds. He places neither at a higher point of value than the other. Emotionalism and emotions should not be equated, any more than we would confuse intellectualism and intellect as being the same. "Ism" moves any subject from its basic essence to become a thing in, of and for itself. "Ism" exaggerates intent, so as healthy emotions are employed in the worship of God, emotional*ism* will disappear, and the health and healing of God's Spirit will be free to move over and among God's people in tender, as well as igniting, ways. Worship is given space to become intermittently passionate and joyful, or quiet and warmly enveloping, being expressed as:

- shouting and clapping hands unto the Lord (Psalm 47:1);
- praising Him aloud with the congregation (Psalm 22:25);
- rejoicing and expressing thanksgiving (Psalm 100:1, 4; Philippians 4:4); and
- being silent before the Lord (Psalm 46:10; Habakkuk 2:20).

As earlier noted, silence as well as shouting may find emotional release. My soul may be tormented and cast about by a thousand pressures on my life, but on my knees and still before Him, I may suddenly become aware: God is on the throne! And being freshly caught up in this awareness, the emotions of peace and confidence, as well as a deep, settled joy in Him, I am freed as I enjoy the blessing of worship—with truly revived, divinely healed and embraced emotions.

With Rededicated Bodies

> Do you not know that your body is the temple of the Holy Spirit who is in you, whom you have from God, and you are not your own? For you were bought at a price; therefore glorify God in your body and in your spirit, which are God's.
>
> 1 Corinthians 6:19–20

In Christ, our human bodies become temples of the Holy Spirit's indwelling, and the gathered congregation at worship becomes a unified building of God by the same term (see Ephesians 2:20–22). The ancient Tabernacle (of Moses) and the Temple (of Solomon) were both proven as places where God's manifest presence visited and where His glory came to reside. "Presenting our bodies" in worship is a commitment intended to open to the same; to open to the Holy Spirit's leading us *after* we worship into lives of obedience and the fulfillment of God's intended purpose for each of us as His created and redeemed sons and daughters. Scripture shows us many ways to praise and worship God with our bodies—now rededicated as temples of His Holy Spirit:

- Kneeling in worship (Philippians 2:9–10)
- Bowed heads (Micah 6:6–8)
- Raised heads (Psalm 3:3–4; Hebrews 4:16)
- Lifted hands (Lamentations 3:40–41; Psalm 63:3–4)
- Waved praise (Leviticus 9:21)
- Dancing with joy before the Lord (Psalm 30:11; 149:3; 150:4)

All of the above, in all four aspects of our being, have offered no more than a pair of references in support of the expression listed. However, there are many more in virtually every instance. And whatever may lack in numerous proof texts, a single chapter demonstrating the power of worship (2 Chronicles 20) reveals no fewer than eleven different verbs that call for our active participation in worship:

> *hadad*—to bend in deference to
> *nafal*—to prostrate before
> *shakah*—to fall before or do homage to royalty
> *halal*—to boast in the Lord
> *gadul*—to call out in a loud voice
> *yadah*—to hold out the hand
> *renah*—to chirp or creak or sing
> *tehelah*—to sing a hymn
> *carach*—to kneel
> *simkah*—to be gleeful
> *samach*—to brighten up

This concentration, backed up by the power-outflow of what occurs in the context, certainly evidences that the Bible's revelation of different physical expressions of worship is not merely an observation of some ancient cultural peculiarities of Jewish worshipers millennia ago. God's Word is eternally applicable as it reveals worship's patterns to us. The only alteration has been in that which Jesus Christ fulfilled of the former Mosaic code and practices that, in type, foreshadowed His perfect and ultimate sacrifice.

"But," inquires someone, "isn't the welcome of such expressions an invitation to confusion by people who randomly and independently intrude their will upon a whole congregation?" And the answer is, "Yes." But that challenge does not alter the call to cultivate worship's full expression. Rather, it calls leaders to teach, to model and to correct or confront aberration. There will be rare cases of people who mistakenly suppose that the true test of spirituality is private spontaneity. While some spontaneity has its place, even it must have some point of discipline and control (see 1 Corinthians 14). The commitment of leadership—pastors, elders—to lead the way in open worship on their own part, will qualify them to speak or correct with authority those who need help in recognizing that liberty is never license, and that a congregation is brought together to worship more as a choir than as a collection of soloists.

I have grown with a congregation taught to move *together* in our singing, our standing, our shouting, our kneeling, our bowing and our praise. This is not intended to oppress anyone, but we make no apology if correction distresses the self-indulgent. "God is not the author of confusion" (1 Corinthians 14:33). Corporate worship means that—*one body* moving forward in worship, greater in strength as a unified body—the whole being greater than the sum of its parts.

People sometimes ask me, "Because The Church On The Way is so large, how can worship be sustained in unity?" The answer is, "More easily than when there were just a few." This is true because the growth of an orderly people of worship forms an increasingly coordinated body—one that, with unity, worships, praises, rejoices and magnifies God, the Father, and glorifies His Son, Jesus Christ, by the power of the Holy Spirit. It is not human regimentation, but a holy release that not only makes worship fulfilling and enjoyable; it also results in the greatest blessing of all as God is glorified.

His manifest presence is in attendance, souls are drawn to Him and many are regularly being born into His Kingdom, as we fulfill "our reasonable service."

Table of Triumph

The Centerpiece of Worship

"Do this in remembrance of Me."

1 Corinthians 11:24

At the center of almost any worship center you will find a table. It may be of the simplest design or may be elaborately conceived and magnificently fashioned. And in the majority of instances, the table will have words either carved or inscribed across the front that faces the gathered worshipers: "In Remembrance of Me."

Whatever it is called in your circle of worship—Communion, Eucharist, mass, the Lord's table—this table is the centerpiece of Christian worship. It has been since the night before the Savior was crucified, when He instituted what has become the ultimate tradition observed by the Church. It was introduced with a simplicity that prevails

until today: (1) involving the basic elements of bread and
wine, testifying to His body and blood; (2) pointing to
continuing observance until He reunites with His own in
the ultimate Kingdom; and (3) attended by worshipful
singing (see Matthew 26:26–30).

In 1 Corinthians 11:23–32, the Holy Spirit has given us
insight into the early Church's way of living out what Jesus
had taught the first disciples. Paul, a come-lately apostle,
describes his own experience of having "received from the
Lord" the pattern of worship he describes. He does not
specify whether he uses this terminology simply to relate
what had been passed to him from Christ via the apostles,
or if he had a visitation from the Savior Himself on some
occasion. In any case, it is to that passage we most
frequently resort to assure an appropriate practice of our
worship at "the Lord's table."

Without laboring to discuss the sometimes-monstrosity
that has been erected around this table—structured by
tradition and often enforced by ecclesiastical authority—I
want to encourage each reader to review the Scriptures in
the simple light of the Gospel of God's grace in Christ. It is,
to me, unimaginable that He ever meant the occasions His
people "remember" the cross to become so encumbered
with religious baggage, restrictions or maudlin habits.

What is it, essentially, that Jesus wants us to "remember"?

My deepest conviction is that Jesus' call to His table is not
to a table of remorse to review His agony, but to a sensitive
yet joyous remembrance of His triumph. The focus of the
cross, from heaven's viewpoint, is doubtless best summarized in Jesus' final words from its crossbars: "It is finished!"
The price of redemption was paid in full! The work of
redemption was completed perfectly! The blood of the
Lamb atoned completely!

The centuries during which the mass was observed as a guilt-inducing repetition of the horror of Jesus' suffering, in sanctuaries where He was still hanging on a cross, served to fix the idea of the table being a morbid time of memorizing details of Christ's ordeal unto death as normal. Peculiarly, even though the Reformation shook loose the chains of bondage to uncertainty regarding one's personal salvation or doubt as to one's standing before God, it seems there has never been a complete liberation of the observance of the table as one of *triumph* rather than *trauma*.

- *Without a doubt*, we *are* called to rehearse the fact of Jesus' broken body and His shed blood:

  > When He had given thanks, He broke it and said, "Take, eat; this is My body which is broken for you; do this in remembrance of Me." In the same manner He also took the cup after supper, saying, "This cup is the new covenant in My blood. This do, as often as you drink it, in remembrance of Me."
  >
  > 1 Corinthians 11:24–25

- *Without a doubt*, we *are* called to retell the Gospel as we tell of His death, keeping in view that God's generous gift of grace did not come cheap, that salvation's dynamic of forgiveness and deliverance was costly, that our need of salvation is underscored by the fact that so great a debt had to be paid, and that the hope of heaven and eternal life has been bequeathed to us at the price of Jesus' suffering unto death, experiencing hell's most violent assault, and rising again to demonstrate the totality of His conquest of death and hell. We are to *declare* these things as we come to His table.

For as often as you eat this bread and drink this cup, you proclaim the Lord's death till He comes.

1 Corinthians 11:26

- **Without a doubt,** Christ's surrender unto death on Calvary is not only a gift bringing us eternal salvation, but also presents us with a discipling model of the life-principle that submission to God's will inevitably requires a death to ourselves—death to any prioritizing of our own convenience or comfort; death to the world and its values, and to the flesh and its lusts.

"Most assuredly, I say to you, unless a grain of wheat falls into the ground and dies, it remains alone; but if it dies, it produces much grain. He who loves his life will lose it, and he who hates his life in this world will keep it for eternal life. If anyone serves Me, let him follow Me."

John 12:24–26

"If anyone desires to come after Me, let him deny himself, and take up his cross, and follow Me. For whoever desires to save his life will lose it, but whoever loses his life for My sake will find it."

Matthew 16:24–25

We are hard pressed on every side, yet not crushed; we are perplexed, but not in despair... always carrying about in the body the dying of the Lord Jesus, that the life of Jesus also may be manifested in our body.

2 Corinthians 4:8, 10

But God forbid that I should boast except in the cross of our Lord Jesus Christ, by whom the world has been crucified to me and I to the world.

Galatians 6:14

Clearly, then, Jesus did intend we learn from His death. But there is a difference in learning a discipling principle and in carrying a weight of unresolved shame or guilt for having been responsible that the Son of God suffered for you. We must decide which of two possibilities motivates His summons—what He has in mind for our mood and manner in coming to His table. We can ask if He has invited us to come to remember the agonizing, viciously cruel process of His dying, and to beat our chests with shame in recurrent acts of self-flagellation for our past and His pain. Or if His intention was that we meet Him at the table to review and celebrate:

- the Father's *purpose* in sending His Son as a love-gift;
- the cross's *power* to break sin and Satan's yoke because He bled and died;
- the promised *provisions* of spiritual wholeness, strength and health because His body was "broken for you"; and
- the *perfected triumph* of His dying, providing full assurance of life abundant now and eternal life forever!

The most natural, and the most biblical and spiritual choice between the two is the latter, because:

1. Jesus Himself is not a psychotic, calling those He has saved to commiserate repeatedly over "the awful suffering I had to endure for you." The Savior is not, if you will, a "Yiddishe Mama," sowing guilt with such words as, "Never let it enter your mind the horrible pain I experienced to see you brought into this world—It's nothing, nothing"; all the while meaning exactly the opposite: "You owe me, and I'll hold it over your head as a means of controlling you forever!!"

2. The Good News of salvation's gift today is not "yesterday's news" of the Savior's suffering to purchase the gift. The fact of His sacrifice is not minimized by proclaiming the liberating intention of His life-gift and His desire that, like the returned prodigal (see Luke 15), we enter into the feast and celebrate our being newly clothed with His righteousness. But "the LORD has anointed Me to preach good tidings . . . to give them beauty for ashes, the oil of joy for mourning, the garment of praise for the spirit of heaviness . . . that He may be glorified" (Isaiah 61:1, 3).

3. The message of life to all who enter the gates of grace is ministered by the Holy Spirit, bringing that order of comfort and confidence heralded by the prophet, saying, " 'Comfort, yes, comfort My people!' says your God. 'Speak comfort to Jerusalem, and cry out to her, that her warfare is ended, that her iniquity is pardoned . . .' " (Isaiah 40:1, 2). This is the Spirit who drew us to Christ, convinced us of our sin, brought us to repentance, regenerated us by His holy power and now brings us to the Savior's table to sup with Him, knowing the welcome of His embrace and the blessing of His daily fellowship as our resurrected Lord.

The process of Jesus' death is obviously of great importance, but the Father's purpose and the Son's provisions to us through His death are accomplished facts for us to receive, to rejoice in and to enjoy without any shadow of guilt or condemnation tainting the glory of His gift—once for all!

> For God did not send His Son into the world to condemn the world, but that the world through Him might be saved.
>
> John 3:17

> There is therefore now no condemnation to those who are in
> Christ Jesus.... For the law of the spirit of life in Christ Jesus
> has made me free from the law of sin and death.
>
> Romans 8:1–2

Let it become fixed forever in every worship leader's mind,
heart, values and style as we come to lead worshipers in
observing the Lord's Supper—He is the One who paid the
price of the feast—He is the One who opens wide the table to
"whosoever will"—He is the One who "was once dead, but
is alive forevermore, and has the keys of death and hell"—
HE IS THE VICTOR, and HIS IS A TABLE OF TRIUMPH!!

FACING DOWN PROBLEM APPROACHES

Sadly, the Lord's table has often become bound by legalism
and used as a whip to control people. There are places in
Christ's global body where Communion is denied as a
means of exacting "discipline." Born-again believers who
have confessed to failure(s)—even though now confessed
and theoretically "forgiven"—are disallowed the privilege
for partaking of the table until pastoral or church authorities allow them to do so.

In many quarters, the table is guarded—visitors disallowed to partake, non-members fended away from
co-observance—in what I am sure must be felt as sincere,
but are nonetheless misguided, unnecessary and unbiblical
prohibitions. The Word of God establishes in Jesus' own
teaching that there is, in fact, something dynamic in
partaking of the Lord's table—"For My flesh is food [spir-
itual nutrition] indeed, and My blood is drink [spiritual
refreshment and life] indeed" (John 6:55). Denying the
ministry of the table to repentant erring believers or saints

who are not members of a given congregation is counter-productive to salvation's purpose and/or biblical Christian fellowship. It is like saying to a starving man, "You'll get something to eat after you get over your malnutrition"; or to a lonely one, "We'll embrace you after you've been around awhile—if you join our club."

Too often has the table of Communion become weighed down with unbiblical teaching that we might place our health or life at risk if we partake "unworthily." This twisted logic comes from 1 Corinthians 11:27–32, where the apostle Paul is prompting self-examination *not* as a means to acquiring sufficient worthiness to justify our coming to Christ's table. Such an idea is ludicrous, given the fact you will *never* find a place in Scripture suggesting we gain or receive anything on the merits of anyone other than Jesus! So what *is* Paul saying?

The sickness or premature death that some Corinthian believers had experienced (see verse 30) was *not* God's judgment on them for partaking of the Lord's Supper without having somehow conditioned themselves to a high enough degree of righteousness. It was because they had forfeited biblical promises of healing and strength, rooted in Jesus' suffering—by whose stripes we are healed! (see Isaiah 53:5; Matthew 8:16; 1 Peter 2:24). They were not being punished, but a significant lesson is nonetheless registered that neutralizes yet another distortion of ensconced teaching in some parts of the Church. The lesson is that *faith* is essential to appropriate the promises of God. And it counters the error that some automatic power is inherent in a mechanical participation in the sacraments.

Let us be done with these points of confusion. And let us come to the table with a holy sobriety, but with a matching spirit of rejoicing.

Let's settle the question once and for all. Who is worthy to come to the table? Nobody. Jesus died to shower the grace of God upon us so that we might all come through *Him* who is worthy. "Worthy is the Lamb," we sing. When I come, I am putting my trust and faith in the Lamb of God who takes away the sin of the world, including the sin of Jack Hayford. I come and partake of His strength, which brings me nourishment. And this is the essence of partaking "in a worthy manner."

We come not on the grounds of our works, though we may rightly expect to come confessing our known sins and points of disobedience or weakness. And having so come, we are called to remember Him—to remember the worthiness of the Lamb of God, who has taken away the sins of the world!

> Let us therefore come boldly to the throne of grace, that we may obtain mercy and find grace to help in time of need.
>
> Hebrews 4:16

We come because *He* is worthy. And on those grounds we have not only been brought before the Father's throne without condemnation, but welcomed to the Son's table without hesitation.

SO WHAT DOES JESUS WANT US TO REMEMBER?

When we come to the Lord's Table, is our Savior seeking to insist we remember how much He suffered on the cross of Calvary as nails pierced His flesh, thorns tore His brow and the spear ripped His side? Does He want us to remember that it was our fault that He had to suffer and die in this cruel way? Does He want us to carry ongoing guilt that will mark us out as His disciples? As worthy and amazingly wondrous the grace that experiences those things, the answer to these questions is no.

Rather, He directs us to come to His table—where we are freed to fellowship with Him because His *did* suffer and He *has* died—and now says, "Rejoice with me!"

- He wants us to remember that His blood was shed once and for all to cover *all* our sin, so that we need never live under condemnation.
- He wants us to remember that when we partake of this bread, like Israel receiving manna in the wilderness, there is supernatural nourishment that provides us with strength for life every day.
- He wants us to remember that He was broken on our behalf to make health possible for us, so that we do not have to endure interminable suffering. Jesus wants us to remember, when we are assaulted by Satan, that He has defeated the adversary and made a spectacle of him—he is a defeated foe.

This is how we discern the Lord's body, which was broken for us—His suffering and death that have established a new covenant through His blood. This is what Jesus wants us to remember—His victory *won* and His battle *complete*.

He invites us to join Him at His table of triumph.

Come! Drink to that!!

CHAPTER 16

Touching Heaven and Earth

The Hands of Worship

Let us lift up our heart with our hands unto God in the heavens.

Lamentations 3:41, KJV

Earlier we examined the fact that the visible and invisible worlds are more closely knit and aligned than our merely human or "natural" mind perceives. Colossians 1 is emphatic that Christ is supreme and that He is Lord of all things "visible and invisible"; a statement that by itself authenticates that neither realm is trivial or unrelated to the whole of our human experience (see verse 16). Accordingly, my convictions about the role that hands play in our life and our worship have only deepened from year to year, and the subject is distinctly important enough to warrant an extended study. Look with me into the spiritual reality linked to such basic physical expressions as (a) raised hands, as declarations of commitment, intercession or blessing; and (b) the clapping of our hands, as a means of exalting God in a way that declares, "Let Your Kingdom come *here*, and Your will be done *here*—as in heaven, so on earth, *here!*" More than we know, the recurrent summons to "lift up your hands" in the Word of God is not simply a cultural callisthenic. It is a means of touching heaven (the invisible) with hands on earth (the visible) and making a "connection" in a way transcending our explanation, but a way known to God—the One far wiser than our diluting and deluding reasonings to the contrary. We can learn more of the relationship between hands of praise and the Hand of All Power—whose Kingdom authority and dominion we so badly need in our world and so whole-heartedly desire in our midst.

THE UPRAISING OF HANDS

The Bible provides lessons on four specific aspects of the purpose of upraised hands.

1. In *confession*: Upraised hands show commitment to the Lord.
2. In *conflict*: Upraised hands determine victory in intercession.
3. In *confrontation*: Upraised hands respond to the loving-kindness of God.
4. In *blessing*: Upraised hands reach out to others with His grace, power and love.

Look with me at each, shown in a biblical case occurring in the lives of some of the great worshipers in history—Abraham, Moses, David and Solomon.

Confession: Acknowledging Whose Side We Are On

The first instance in the Bible of hands being raised in the name of the Lord takes place with Abraham, who lifts his hands as a confession of his commitment to the Lord: "Abram said to the king of Sodom, 'I have raised my hand to the LORD, God Most High, the Possessor of heaven and earth'" (Genesis 14:22).

When he speaks these words, Abraham is returning from battle, having rescued his nephew Lot and others who had been taken captive from Sodom by a group of kings from the surrounding nations. As they make their way home, Abraham is confronted by the pagan king of Sodom who wants the people returned, for which he will allow Abraham to keep the goods he has gained. By raising his hands to the Lord, Abraham makes it clear which side he is on, refusing to be identified with that which is alien to the way of the Lord.

Like so many great principles in the Bible, the simple hermeneutic of the Law of First Usage established upraised hands as being dramatically significant. Further, Romans 4:12–16 notes Abraham as the spiritual "father" of New Testament believers just as he is the natural *paterfamilia* of the Jews. Being instructed to "walk in the steps of the faith of our father Abraham," a readiness to express our commitment to God with upraised hands is more than merely reasonable. It's a biblically confirmed sign of abiding commitment.

Conflict: Gaining Victory in Spiritual Warfare

The stretching forth of Moses' hands provides us with one of the greatest examples of intercessory prayer in the Bible (see Exodus 17). While the battle against the Amalekites is raging in the valley below, Moses stands on the hill, along with Aaron and Hur, with his arms raised holding his rod in his hands: "And so it was, when Moses held up his hand, that Israel prevailed; and when he let down his hand, Amalek prevailed" (verse 11).

All the while Moses raised his rod up high, Israel had the upper hand in the battle. After a time his arms became so heavy that he sat down on a huge stone, and Aaron and Hur supported his hands in the air. By the raising of his hands Moses determined whether or not the victory would be won. Perhaps the greatest summons in the Bible to intercessory prayer (see 1 Timothy 2:1–8) is sealed with upraised hands: "I desire therefore that the men pray everywhere, lifting up holy hands, without wrath and doubting" (verse 8).

Someone once used the fact that this is the only specific allusion to upraised hands in the New Testament to ask me about the practice's validity. I replied, "Well, how many texts do you need?" When the Lord speaks, once is enough. Paul asks all "men" (generic) "everywhere" to lift up holy hands in intercession. Those who seek victory in intercessory prayer will raise their hands to the Lord.

Confrontation: Offering Praise No Matter the Trial

At a time when David is in the wilderness of Judah, running for his life, he sings this lyric to the Lord: "Because Your lovingkindness is better than life, my lips shall praise You. Thus I will bless You while I live; I will lift up my hands in Your name" (Psalm 63:3–4; see also 1 Samuel 21–25).

To understand the context of these verses, is to realize how tender they are. Despite his facing the likelihood of death at any moment, David chooses to lift his voice and his hands to the Lord. Regardless of what he's going through, David continues to affirm that the Lord's loving-kindness never changes—that He is *always* worthy of our praise. Reaching to God with upraised hands in times of trial, but with songs of praise, is an invitation to His almightiness to lift us beyond our trial into His place of soul-rest and inner confidence. Like David, we need to confront the things that would distress us beyond measure, threatening our very well-being, and keep lifting up, praising God.

Blessing: Reaching Out to Others

On the occasion of the dedication of the Temple, Solomon prays a magnificent prayer commending the ways of his people to the Lord, following which we read:

> And so it was, when Solomon had finished praying all this prayer and supplication to the LORD, that he arose from before the altar of the LORD, from kneeling on his knees with his hands spread up to heaven. Then he stood and blessed all the assembly of Israel with a loud voice.
>
> 1 Kings 8:54–55

The Hebrew word *barak* means to bless—with the lexicon specifically interpreting to us that the word incorporates the idea of one's "extending of hands." Having raised his hands to heaven, Solomon then extends his hands in blessing over his people. The back-to-back employment of his hand, first upraised toward God in intercession and then extended forth in an act of blessing toward others, is a profound pairing of gestures. The spiritual significance dare not be overlooked. Hands that come out of the presence of the Living God can be extended to others in life and grace, as Jesus promised they would when He said, "These signs will follow those who believe . . . they will lay hands on the sick, and they will recover" (Mark 16:17–18).

Let us understand the wisdom of our lifting hands before God because we need the touch of God upon them. If this were the only reason, it would be reason enough. Indeed, upraised hands are a fundamental part of our turning to the Lord, as the writer of Lamentations declares: "Let us search out and examine our ways, and turn back to the LORD; let us lift our hearts and hands to God in heaven" (Lamentations 3:40–41).

CLAPPING OF HANDS:
PROPRIETY AND PROBLEM

Apart from singing, it is likely that today's second most frequent physical expression of worship in the global Church community is the clapping of hands. Like the upraising of hands, the clapping of hands is an instrument of praise and of spiritual warfare, as well as an appropriate gesture for the welcome of royalty. Psalm 47:1 is doubtless the verse most quoted on the subject: "Oh, clap your hands, all you peoples! Shout to God with the voice of triumph!" The text not only legitimizes the practice as a part of our worship, it exhorts us to employ applause to God. The psalm continues:

For the LORD Most High is awesome;
He is a great King over all the earth.
He will subdue the peoples under us,
And the nations under our feet....
God has gone up with a shout,
The LORD with the sound of a trumpet....
God reigns over the nations;
God sits on His holy throne.

verses 2–3, 5, 8

This is a declarative acknowledgment that He is mighty, awesome and glorious; and that He is disposed to our favor, moving into His place of enthronement as we praise Him *right now*. Our worship and praise are dynamic, not because of the energy of flesh, but because of the fruit they bear. A place is made for the Lord to come, dwell and move among His people in glory and power (see Psalm 22:3).

As we respond appropriately to the majesty and goodness of who God is, what He has done and the blessing of His Person in our midst, He responds by moving among us in greater dimension, bringing His glory, radiance and transformation. This in turn begets from us more praise, giving Him more room to dwell, and thus the cycle continues. It is the very scene of the throne room of heaven where endless praise is going forth (see Revelation 4). It is the order of eternity, which has as its outflow the ongoing, creative action of almighty God who works creatively and redemptively wherever people praise Him without ceasing.

All this clearly indicates more than the propriety of the clapping of hands among believers as we worship the Living God; it virtually suggests that to do otherwise is *im*proper! But it is possible that some may be reticent today because it is unquestionable that too frequently hand clapping is disorderly, meaninglessly redundant or mind-lessly offered as habit.

For example, to note the directive in Psalm 47:1 is to see it *unites* the clapping of hands with verbalized praise. Of course, it isn't wrong to clap our hands without verbalizing praise, nor to verbalize praise without clapping our hands. Yet it is significant and observable with disappointing frequency that in a setting where people are worshiping the Lord, once applause begins, verbalized praise tends to cease. To my observation, the applause tends to substitute for thoughtful expressions of worship when it is best that the two be combined as the Word declares.

Further, hand clapping has become something of an "anytime" means of putting a "tag" or conclusion on some-thing that occurs in a service. This isn't necessarily bad—in fact, it is often very appropriate. But as with all ritual, as we have discussed, whatever becomes mindlessly exercised becomes spiritually vacuous.

How Applause Is Used with Understanding

We see at least four biblical principles in action when we worship with the clapping of our hands:

1. the declaration of victory and joy,
2. the expression of approval or affirmation,
3. the establishment of covenant or the sealing of an agreement, and
4. the engaging of a powerful instrument of spiritual warfare.

The Declaration of Victory and Joy

To "make a joyful noise" is an expression of clapping hands. A cluster of texts affirms this practice:

- "shout" and "make His praise glorious" (Psalm 66:1, 2);
- "shout ... and strike the timbrel" (Psalm 81:1, 2);
- "people who know the joyful sound" (Psalm 89:15);
- "shout joyfully" as rivers "clap their hands" (Psalm 98:4–6, 8);
- "gather us ... to triumph in Your praise" (Psalm 106:47).

The Bible affirms and directs *triumph* in praise, and human experience confirms that the most common expression celebrating victory, honoring achievement and or declaring triumph is with exclamations and the clapping of our hands. It is the most natural thing for people who are happy to clap their hands; just look at what a child does in a spontaneous expression of delight. The evidence of the Word and our God-given natural tendencies when rejoicing support this liberating practice. Joyful expression lauding the glorious goodness of God often recommends the clapping of hands; it is spiritual, scriptural and appropriate.

The Expression of Our Approval or Affirmation
In 2 Kings 11 the story is told of how, when King Ahaziah died, his mother killed all the heirs to the throne in a bid to take it for herself. Joash, however, was spared and was hidden away for six years until at the age of seven he was made king. On the occasion of his coronation, the people clapped in approval at the establishment of God's king (see verse 12). In the same way, we affirm the Kingship of our Lord Jesus Christ by clapping our hands. By applauding, we are welcoming royalty into our midst and welcoming the King into His place of rightful rule.

The Establishment of Covenant or Agreement

Just as in our modern culture we shake hands in agreement, in the culture of ancient Israel they struck hands to indicate agreement or a closed contract. In a negative example, Proverbs 17:18 and 22:26 (KJV) refer to the foolishness of agreeing to guarantee someone else's debts by striking or clapping hands. A positive example is seen in Job 17:3 where he is looking for someone who will stand with him and asks, "Who is he that will strike hands with me?" In Scripture the striking of hands is a sign of making a covenant. By clapping our hands, we confirm our striking a covenant with God's promises to us; or, receiving a prophetic "word," we clap our hands to affirm our readiness to appropriate the truth that prophecy reflects from "the Word."

The Engaging of an Instrument of Spiritual Warfare

The clapping of hands is a weapon of spiritual warfare, somehow effective as an instrument that drives back the enemy. In this way we are applying applause as it was sometimes used in the Old Testament as a sign of derision, contempt or mocking. In Lamentations 2:15, while prophesying about Jerusalem's destruction, Jeremiah says: "All who pass by clap their hands at you; they hiss and shake their heads at the daughter of Jerusalem." Similar examples appear in Ezekiel 25:6 and Nahum 3:19, as well as in Job 27:23 where, in speaking about the evil one, he says: "Men shall clap their hands at him, and shall hiss him out of his place." By clapping our hands, we employ one of the arsenals of spiritual weapons, which transcend the natural, visible realm and make the Kingdom advance against dark powers in the spiritual, invisible realm.

A Personal Testimony of Applause in Spiritual Warfare

Not long after Anna and I took the pastorate of the congregation later to be called The Church On The Way, I encountered a challenge that at first only seemed "human" in its nature. Without my seeking a supernatural explanation for the obstacles we faced, the Holy Spirit graciously drew me to discover the source of the spiritual blockage: It was a hideous demonic oppression that existed in that place. To suggest that there are spirits of oppression that have to do with buildings can sound superstitious and bizarre to some people, but there is no question that such things do occur.

At first, I merely "felt" something peculiar in the room at times, but I never spoke a word to anyone about this until one day when a solid, tough-minded, non-superstitious working man in that small congregation said something to me. He was the only remaining member of the church board when we inherited that handful of 18 people, and one evening he acknowledged his sense of a terrible presence. He noted with me how that "thing" seemed to weigh in with an oppression against anything that God led the people to do. It wasn't his comments that brought it to my awareness, however. The first time I came into the room I felt it.

Further, peculiar things happened from time to time (and apparently had been happening before I arrived); for example, flashing lights, unexplained sudden blackouts (that were more than electrical failures), shadowy presences. Besides those occasional, though not constant irregularities, I found myself "chilled" when walking through the sanctuary after turning out the lights and having to walk a short distance to the door with only slight ambient streetlight to show the way. Quite uncharacteristically, I became afraid when I was there in the dark.

As for manifestations in services, the primary one was a near indefinable, but very real, barricade to worship that seemed to be raised *every time* we began a service. It wasn't the people: They were gracious and cooperative. But any expression of joy or praise was difficult to come by, unity was hard to generate: It was somewhat as a barren womb—there was no *life* in the atmosphere. Moving through one of our services during that early season at the church was something of a wrestling match. I never surrendered to it, because we would patiently persist in song and praise until a loosening occurred. But a few months after I came, something happened.

What I learned to do might seem a little strange, but I have found that the strength of our church body's life does not come from trying to seem sophisticated but simply from teaching principles that the Lord invites us as children to respond to.

I used to come in the side door of the sanctuary—you could not come in the front door because it unlocked from the inside. And it was one morning as I entered that the Holy Spirit allowed me a vision, with an accompanying direct impression giving the understanding that a demonic presence had been given place to in that sanctuary long before. I have no idea how that happened, and have never made any charges or suggestions as to who or what was the root of this embedded bondage to the atmosphere in that small sanctuary. But from that day (without telling anyone in the congregation what I had been shown) whenever I entered the sanctuary alone, I would begin to clap my hands and sing praises.

It was clear to me that praise to God is given as a spiritual weapon that can be leveled against spiritual oppression.

> For the weapons of our warfare are not carnal but mighty in God for pulling down strongholds, casting down ... every high thing that exalts itself against the knowledge of God.
>
> 2 Corinthians 10:4–5

During times I was alone in the building, I made a practice of often shouting the name of Jesus with exalted and high praise, singing with the understanding and with the Spirit, and attending all this with clapping my hands— laying hold of the triumph of Jesus' cross over the enemy, according to the Word of God (see Psalm 47:1; Colossians 2:14–15).

It did not seem necessary or, at that time, appropriate to even tell anyone of my actions. There are some things the Spirit shows a person that are to be acted upon, not spoken to others. Such was my sense on that matter at that time. But today I retell the story here, just as in the chapter on "The Leprous House" in my book *Worship His Majesty* (Regal Books—Ventura, California). Without further elaboration, suffice it to say my challenge of that "barricade" in the spiritual realm realized an eventual victory after a number of months of the intercession I have described. And from that time on, the church grew in our experience of worship and in the realizing of the manifest presence of God.

I end with that testimony, not to leave you with a melodramatic story. But to illustrate a reality, and to remind us all of a fundamental fact. God seeks to bless *all* His people, but He is most free to do so with those who understand and respond to His ways and His Word—with those who are most ready to worship Him openly, freely and with that childlikeness only a simple faith in the spiritual nature of His Word will bring.

As we have looked at the simplicity of principles related to the raising and clapping of our hands, I want to emphasize that I am not proposing formulas or magic exercises. Never! But these *are* biblically ordered forms of worship which, when applied with biblical wisdom and spiritual understanding, hold great potential as keys to the release of God's power among and through His people. They are forms of worship that remain timeless and eternal for all God's people—a companion means for welcoming the majesty of the King into our presence, that His splendor and rule may be enthroned among us and His glory be known to the nations . . .

. . . and our neighborhood.

CHAPTER 17

Decently and in Order

Leading Others in Worship

What establishes an atmosphere for worship?

It's a worthy question, because the truth is that disorder is not an atmosphere conducive to inviting anyone into your setting, much less the Living God. For just as habits of self-evolved rigidity in service structures or personal reserve may obstruct an open-hearted approach to God, so may habits of obvious or undiscerned disorder block our best pursuits in worship. Church order is not a new problem, born of contemporary actions or attitudes; it is also a problem that the early Church was called to address.

The dilemma facing the church at Corinth was not in its exercise of the gifts of the Spirit but in its ignorance of knowing how to fit things together in a service so that its worship would be edifying. In seeking to help them resolve it, the apostle Paul outlines principles of order for worship, that to this day still provide a biblical grid for self-analysis. First Corinthians 14:26–40 still points the way toward establishing a climate of open worship, disciplined by a governing mentality, rooted in a maxim that speaks across the centuries as a golden rule for church worship gatherings: "Let all things be done decently and in order" (verse 40).

The Greek word *euskemonos*, translated "decently," has to do with aesthetics and propriety, conveying a union of the ideas of beauty and graciousness in form or execution. The purpose in its use by Paul was certainly not a proposal to "craft" services so as to make them an art form or mere study in style, nor to "control" them to the point of imposing human obstacles to the presence or movement of the Holy Spirit. Rather, Paul calls us to a standard of *conduct*—to principles that balance the involvement of the congregation in response to God's presence, under the leadership of elders who are conscientious to keep a focus on both edifying values and evangelistic sensitivity.

To the beauty and grace of "decently," is added "order"—*taxis* being the New Testament Greek word in this case. It has to do with sequence or occurrence, under-lining the idea of each thing having "its proper place according to its nature." Hence our word *taxonomy*, the word used to title the science of classifying all things of flora and fauna in the world of biology. And thus "decently" and "in order" combine to call us to sense the Holy Spirit, and to govern with enlightened hearts as we seek to offer our corporate worship as congregations, led in wisdom and with humility, so that basic beauty of conduct and dignity of order worthy of our entry before God's throne result in gatherings that are comforting, encourag-ing and edifying to all in attendance.

POINTS OF LEADERSHIP DISCERNMENT AND DECISION

With the essential meaning of those words in view, let me touch briefly on several factors, which, while not directly related to the exercise of worship itself, are still fundamental to deciding the climate, atmosphere and attitude of worship in a church. Consider how the following factors call each of us who lead worship to points of discerning decision.

A. Motivating Concept

The "planned" nature of church services, as contrasted with private worship or small group gatherings, requires a discerning answer to these questions: Have the leaders developed a philosophy of "doing church"? Or do gatherings simply "happen from habit," on the supposition that everyone simply "knows" why we're doing this and how we ought to go about it? Is worship designed to lead people into the presence of God in ways that attract all present to unite with understanding as hearts open to Him? Or are gatherings essentially tailored as an effective production, designed more to invite people into "this room," and not necessarily press the issue of leading them into heaven's throne room?

What is your disposition as a leader toward "church"? Is it essentially an "event," or an "entry"? Is the desire motivating the assembly to gather intended to facilitate growth and development in the body life of the church? Or is it essentially to attract—to appeal to people; to draw a crowd? It is an important point of difference, because the idea of designing gatherings suited foremost to answer to "human favor" will eventually lead to merely growing a crowd rather than growing a people who learn the wonder

and power of the presence of God. We can beget "nice" or
even "great" services, but in the last analysis I, as a leader,
have to answer as to how often I lead gatherings that realize
divine encounters.

Attracting larger numbers of people is not an unworthy
objective. Outreach calls for strategies designed to do that.
But sooner or later, I, as a leader, am called to decide
whether I am willing to discern the difference between
(a) an event planned for "celebrating God" (with quality
music and upbeat praise), and (b) a gathering intended for
"encountering God" (with effective musical support, praise
[upbeat] as an *entry* into His presence, and worship [probing
and sensitive] as an *exposure* to His Person. Thus, there is
an atmosphere to be decided upon. As a leader, I need to
answer the question: What degree of worship, or full
exposure to the presence and power of God do I want to
plan toward leading those I serve?

B. Order and Decorum

The matters of order and decorum in church services is too
seldom valued or evaluated in many settings. Regarding
"order," there are amazingly insensitive concessions
commonly made to disruptions. Unruly or untended children, people who move about randomly, confused notions
of "spiritual liberty" and other such issues are often
endured or tolerated by leaders. A gathering for worship
and edification is not a "front room in my house" experience and doesn't require permitting "whatever" in the
name of hospitality. At the same time, rigidity, legalistic
mandates and loveless administration are suffocating.

What atmosphere does your church family want to have
in your church home? It's up to each to decide, and it isn't

my call to prescribe what everybody should do. However, through the years we have discovered that it is possible to (a) welcome a liberating presence of the Holy Spirit, (b) embrace a generous hospitality toward visitors and all others present (including visitor's children), (c) celebrate openly and boldly the glories of the King, and (d) humbly and with sensitive reverence and availability to God's awesome presence, give place to *order* and *God's power*—all at the same time, in the same worship service.

Decorum references "propriety, good taste, conduct or appearance, behavior consistent with normal self-respect or humane feeling for others." To even write these words puts me at risk as being more concerned with "man-pleasing" than with "God-pleasing" in the view of some who suppose the truly spiritual gathering to be defined by an ungoverned sloppiness that is without any regard to just plain thoughtfulness.

Again, I will not presume to define another congregation's "right or wrong" practices for them. But I have witnessed too many outright, though oft self-righteous indulgences that violate taste. But let me be clear: I am not proposing an ultimate "ecclesiastical liturgy," but I would urge churches everywhere to regularly reassess what accumulated insensitivities may have been garnered with time. How warmly are people *really* greeted? What appearance does the platform and its occupants present, indicating that "God is the primary guest here"? Some think that such matters have nothing to do with spirituality, but I disagree. Human beings can be sorely distracted from what a leader (not to mention *God*) is trying to accomplish if that leader is not sensitive to what the mood and manner of the platform, and the sensitivity and structure of the proceedings, convey to the people.

Decorum is important, not to impress people with our style, but to avoid distressing them by our shoddiness; to avoid distractions and to help those present to focus their attention on the real goals of the service.

C. Condition of Church Facilities

Another issue that affects the climate of worship is the upkeep and general appearance of the building (or buildings) in which the church meets. If the facilities are untidy, neglected or even occasionally dirty, they can, at the very least, be another distraction. In some instances, moreover, without unduly spiritualizing the matter, the confusion of the situation may have a spiritual dimension. I have personally discipled pastors who were struggling in situations of utter chaos and disorder, and together we discovered that they were not dealing with flesh and blood in the material realm. When finally they dealt with the spiritual dimension of the problem, there came breakthrough and the realization of the grace of God, which brought a new order and beauty to the situation.

Twice, I've pastored small congregations in unimpressive buildings. And I've learned the maxim, "It's what you do with what you've got," to worthily apply in this regard. In the final analysis, atmosphere will not be determined by how elegant a gathering place, but by how excellent the preparation and use of what you *do* have are cared for and prepped for each gathering.

D. Exercise of Gifts of the Holy Spirit

Consideration also needs to be given to house rules on the exercise of the spiritual gifts. As I've said on other matters above, I do not believe my opinion to be conclusively right, though we have learned satisfactory procedures that both honor the Scriptures and bring release to worshipers.

A congregation's primary leadership must reach a point of mutual determination and agreement on this. Since the Bible says that the gifts of the spirit of the prophets are subject to the prophets, I conclude it essentially provides a level of local autonomy—a choice of *what* spirit—be it holy and beautiful, human and acceptable; or carnal and self-serving, demonic or bizarre, that which is religiously plastic and theatrically sensational.

First Corinthians 14 gives a broad outline of principles for thoughtful self-discipline and maintained clarity of purpose where the gifts of the Spirit are welcomed in public services. Our elders have embraced these principles deeply and with commitment. We believe the Holy Spirit is to be welcomed in all our services, feeling that preempting Him from any gathering by imposed regulations is presumptuous. Better, to our view, is to learn how to govern by *His* rules—just as they are revealed in the Bible. Sometimes His rules confront human exaggeration or unnecessary display. When that happens, gentle, well-explained correction secures order, but loving and pastoral ways of doing so preserve the spirit of a holy liberty for members to minister gifts as the Spirit chooses to distribute them on some occasion of public gathering.

WORSHIP PROBLEMS IN THE BIBLE

It takes preparation to move a service toward form, order, dignity, decorum and loveliness. The reason a service does not just fall into place—especially when it comes to worship—is because we are often dealing with human slowness and resistance to change. These may not be calculated, but even among the most sincere believers they reflect human nature. But we face more than the potential of human resistance. When it comes to such crucial issues as the power of God breaking forth upon a people, we can count on satanic opposition or a manifest spirit of religious confusion sooner or later.

At least four examples in Scripture illustrate worship gone wrong:

- Only four chapters into Genesis, we find in Cain the first example of resistance to worship and unwilling-ness to accept the divine order.
- Seven chapters later, in Genesis 11, the Tower of Babel demonstrates the human attempt to use architecture rather than humility in worship as access to an effective approach to God. Might this delusion still find place in any environment where we think a better building will be the key to our success, or that merely polishing up the sanctuary is what prepares a place for meeting God? While buildings and a readied auditorium are not unimportant, preoccupation with structural forms can be delusions.
- In Numbers 3:4, Nadab and Abihu attempt to offer "profane fire before the LORD," instead of God's pre-scribed formula for the incense that was to be offered in Israel's worship. Their folly led to divinely forewarned and disastrous results. Similarly, we would be well warned to discern our own potential for offering "strange fire" to God. There *are* biblical guidelines and practices, principles and inviolable concepts fundamental to New Testament worship. To violate

them may not produce dead bodies, but it can result in a congregation that is a "dead body." Our "fire" is no substitute for "fire from on high"—the outpouring of the Holy Spirit, shed upon a people who exalt Jesus Christ, who honor the Word of God and who meet to encounter Him—not to exercise their own agenda.

- Exodus 32 unfolds the devastatingly deadly account of Aaron's horrific mishandling of his priestly assignment. He conceded to the preferences of his congregation and erected the golden calf *by his hand* because it was demanded *by his congregation's tastes.* How painfully the episode demonstrates a leader's shaping worship to suit the demands of a people, rather than by teaching and leading them patiently, faithfully and with biblical authority to worship God as He has called us to worship and to serve Him.

AVOIDING DEADENING RITUALS

There is no merit in any activity if we do not understand what we are doing and why we are doing it. Without careful teaching, practices become meaningless, habitual responses no longer energized with life. They are not necessarily the byproducts of hardness of heart or bitterness toward God; they can simply be the result of lack of effective leadership.

Jesus said, quoting from the book of Isaiah, "These people draw near to Me with their mouth, and honor Me with their lips, but their heart is far from Me" (Matthew 15:8).

A wise leader will consistently assist and alert his people to help them avoid yielding to the syndrome of lip worship without heart worship. The problem is potential to the best and most sincere among us. A good insight regarding the Bible's guideline for avoiding deadening rituals is seen in God's directive concerning Israel's celebration of the Passover. Parents were instructed to teach their children why the ritual was being undertaken; to do so, their worship prompted a "Why?" from the children. As simple as the record may seem, it is a divine warning against practices of worship that can too easily become meaningless responses or empty forms. Any of us can go through the motions of a form and miss out on the substance.

One of the things that characterized my own exposure to worship, in my classical Pentecostal background, is what I eventually termed "the seventeen-second syndrome." Seventeen seconds (though I never actually timed it) was the approximate amount of time it took from an invitation to concerted public praise by the congregation to the moment their verbal praise trailed off to silence. Usually one person or part of the group characteristically sustained praise louder and longer than the rest; it was a good deal less than a half-minute. The problem this reflected to me was not in either the duration or volume of the praise, but in the fact that a *habit* of praise, however sincere the intent, became so perfunctory and conditioned a response that there was a predictable length of its sustainment.

More than anything reflected in this was that the ritual suggested an absence of focus, though there was a continuance of tradition. In short, it was good that "we praised God out loud and together in our church." But what was not good was that a predictable length virtually verified an absence of fresh, conscious subject matter as the *reason* for the praise. In short, the reason had become the activity, not the Person we worship or the specific blessings freshly deserving His praise.

Of course, even to observe as much subjects one to the possibility of being considered critical or judgmental. I am being neither, but I am seeking to point each of us who lead to the need for helping those we lead in worship to do more than "go through the motions."

Scripture further speaks of the excess baggage that can accumulate around worship. The moneychangers in the Temple and the Pharisees' attitude toward the Sabbath are two classic examples in Jesus' ministry (for example, see Matthew 12; Luke 13; John 2). In the minds of the Jews, both of these issues were central to worship. Theoretically, the moneychangers were there to facilitate worship by enabling local and foreign arrivals on the Temple grounds to use a common currency. The passion of the religious leaders for the Sabbath was, to their ideology, a passion to secure appropriate honor of God's commandment as they had come to interpret its requirements. But both these matters had become locked up—bound and tied by human tradition. That's the reason Jesus overturned the moneychangers' tables, and also why He argued with forcible logic in confronting those who challenged His application of the principle of the Sabbath. It provoked such a reaction that people wanted to take His life on the spot!

One more case in point is how the Corinthians exercised the beautiful benefit of speaking with tongues, but abused its purpose with the intrusion of a spiritual habit into a setting where many present were either unaware of this precious gift's value, or where unbelievers would be perplexed by their words and distracted from finding the Lord. That observation is important, but Paul's words should never be confused as being a disapproval of speaking with tongues. A simple read of the whole of 1 Corinthians 14 secures the fact that this was valued and had a proper place in each believer's life, both to Paul's perspective and in the apostolic Church in general.

Each of these biblical examples demonstrates that the intrusion of problems in worship gatherings are not peculiar to our own era. They have happened throughout the ages, and wise leaders find ways of solving them rather than neglecting or avoiding them for fear of the responsibility, or the response, of those taught or corrected.

SENSITIVITY TO THE SEASONS

I urge pastoral and local congregational leaders—especially senior pastors—to think beyond the "this particular service" mind-set. In teaching, I am always mindful that this one meeting is an incremental part of a larger discipling program I am pursuing with the people I serve. Each service is unique, of course. And there are days that are *carpe deim* occasions— a day to be seized in God's timing and purpose. But sensitivity to the seasons (a) of a congregation's larger formation, and (b) to what Christ is doing in His Church in your city, your fellowship of churches, your nation, our world—is essential, and each worship service deserves to be held in that larger context as a leader sees it. Yes, there are times of special breakthrough; yes, there are near-explosive moments of divine release. But in the ongoing life of a congregation, the things that shape the life of that church usually happen over periods of time—three to six weeks, or two to three months; increments of time during which the Holy Spirit speaks, moves, leads and ministers. A leader's sensitivity to Him is essential.

Referencing seasons or holiday occasions such as

Christmas and Easter times, summer vacation, September's return-to-home-and-school mentality, New Year's ready-to-make-a-fresh-start attitude—these all are more than cultural moments; they are potential spiritual opportunities to correlate human readiness at a natural level with spiritual realities at the eternal plane. It is not a matter of attempting to dictate to God that He should do thus-and-so because it's (for example) Christmastime. But we would be wise to recognize *He* understands our creature-hood: "For He knows our frame; He remembers that we are dust" (Psalm 103:14). God knows that different seasons on earth, whether climatic or cultural, take on different points of emotional, physical, mental reference. Don't be surprised that He will guide the sensitive leader on how to maximize the possibility of employing "seasons" to develop the hearts and lives of His people.

LEADERSHIP POINTERS

1. Sensitive, Spiritually Discerning Variety in Approach

It is important for us to avoid the trap of worshiping God in the same way every time we come together. Sometimes we kneel, sometimes we clap our hands, sometimes we sing in the Spirit, but we will not necessarily do any or all these things on every occasion. This is not altered for novelty, but direction is sought in prayer.

How, you may ask, can it be determined what is appropriate for the situation? Sometimes we will not know until we are in the situation and the Holy Spirit prompts us. Generally, however, as we pray for a service and ask God in which direction He wants to lead us, He will begin to direct us. When we have discovered the general direction that the service should take, we can begin to think more specifically about the practice of worship that will contribute to that objective.

In preparing for a service, we need to ask three questions:

1. What is the Lord saying that this service is to be about?
2. What is the Lord doing at this time in our church?
3. What pattern of use (or undue repetition) have we made of any particular piece of music or expression of praise?

Variations in communication and/or expression are essential. What we say while leading people should not become sloganized. All communication should be with integrity—no throwaway lines, trite or cute remarks, but rather, "If anyone speaks, let him speak as the oracles of God" (1 Peter 4:11). The limited time a worship service allows for shaping, discipling, comforting or evangelizing is too precious to waste. Even humor, while very desirable, must be measured lest it trivialize the eternal or become an end in itself. The frequency with which different exercises in worship are employed is governed by what the Holy Spirit is giving in perspective on that service. In my pastoral setting we lead in ways that tend to beget verbal praise as well as song, and upraised hands as well as joyous, uplifted heads in virtually every service. Those expressions are constant. But beyond what I have already written regarding the physical expressions of worship, the following additional considerations regarding variation of approach may provide helpful guidelines.

2. A Practical Sensibility in the Selection of Worship Music

Our worship music needs to be varied. Leaders need to be asking themselves, "Are we singing a song frequently right now because it is fortifying something the Holy Spirit is saying to the church? Is it a song we have just learned that we want to establish in the repertoire of the congregation? Or is it a song we have sung so many times that we ought to declare a moratorium on it for a while?"

From my observation, there is usually not more than one song a year that is introduced into the life of the church that really has ongoing durability. Certain songs are possessed with a timeless quality and will be sung for years to come. But there have been hundreds upon hundreds of good choruses that have come, served well for a period of time and then gone. They are prophetic in the sense that they are "in part,"—that is, born of the Spirit "for a season." However, wise leadership discerns when such a song overstays its spiritual usefulness and becomes a "dead letter" instead of a "living word," working against what it was earlier used by the Lord to achieve.

It is very important to have a prayerful and studied inflow of new songs. Eight times the Scripture says, "Sing unto the Lord a new song," and amid the profusion of worship music from the global Church family, it becomes the leaders' responsibility to find and utilize those which will invigorate and bring freshness to the worship life of the church.

3. Servant-Hearted Partnership with Worship Singers and Musicians

Cooperation between the worship team and the pastor is of fundamental importance. There are a number of different possibilities and combinations in the constitution of the worship team. Whatever the arrangement of the musicians and singers, it is the responsibility of the principal leader of the congregation to be in touch with that group, meeting with them regularly in prayer and discussing what the Holy Spirit is saying to the church at this time. If that is not happening, then the pastor is forfeiting coming to terms with what the priority of worship is in the life of the church.

It may seem very spiritual for the pastor to say that he trusts the worship team. But it is not a matter of trust; it is one of spiritually, lovingly and servant-heartedly *governing*. It is a matter of being in touch together with what the Lord is doing in the church, and that is integral to the responsibility of the congregation leader. Consultation and discussion between pastor and worship team must be part of the worship life of the church.

There is a wide range of specifics to be discussed between pastor and team; I will mention just a few. How will transitions in the service be handled? How will introductions both to songs and to other parts of the service be managed? How will new songs be introduced? How will the service end? All these things are very important to the flow of a service. The congregation will gauge quickly if the approach is haphazard, which in turn will affect their response.

The coordination of a worship service may seem merely of psychological significance, but if these aspects are not attended to, they will distract from the task of worship. It is not about giving the service a professional gloss, but about doing everything possible to enable people to worship God fully. We are dealing with human nature. I am not even talking about fallen human nature, but about the way people function psychologically. A failure to attend to these matters will be counterproductive to what the church is seeking to accomplish in worship. It is safe to say that it will also impede the work of the Holy Spirit because He has given the pastor the task of leadership in these matters. We need to seek to achieve a structure that will help the people respond and move together with a sense of smoothness, orderliness and loveliness, and it is worth the time it takes in working with the musicians to achieve it.

In this same regard, let me address the need for giving careful consideration to the role of choirs. Choirs and special music can easily dominate a service. In the worship life of the people of Israel, choirs were never intended for the purpose of performance. *The choir was not meant to substitute for the praise of the people of the Lord but to stimulate it.* We have moved to the opposite pole, and the music department easily becomes, as the old way puts it, the "war department" of the church. This is more than a cute comment; it is a spiritual challenge to guard against. The music ministry is the most likely place to expect the adversary, and this should come as no surprise: Lucifer was the worship leader of the universe until he lost his position (see Isaiah 14). No wonder worship can become such a contested issue! He is still untiring in his efforts to distract from the worship of God, and to "get all the attention on me . . . or else!"

Whatever activity is undertaken in worship, I am always greatly disturbed if it becomes a private clique of the elite— the protected domain of a small group of gifted people who have little patience with less talented, or people other than themselves. True worship leaders—musicians and singers— will cultivate ministry in others as a means of sharing their gifts, not protecting them.

4. Increasing Congregational Participation

I am persuaded that the foremost key to leading a people—a
congregation, a whole church body—into vital worship
is by prayerful, passionate planning and a virtually des-
perate pursuit of God. At the bottom line, the worship
leadership (the pastor leading the way) needs to spend time
in both prayerful and careful preparation for the service.

In my experience, this involves three or four of the
primary team seeking to discern what the Lord wants to
do this time among those of His people we are privileged
to lead. I am convinced that this is pivotal in begetting a
willingness and responsiveness among the congregation.
Central to that occurring is that, even before the people
gather, there is value and passion manifest for them before
God.

In the early days of my pastorate at The Church On The
Way, when there were about fifty to sixty people in the
congregation, I used to spend time on Saturday evenings
preparing for the service. I would pray in the sanctuary of
the church, praying briefly over every seat, and while doing
so would move through the room asking the Lord to
sensitize my heart. I wanted to know *His* heart for each
individual who would be gathering for worship. "Lord," I
prayed, "let us not miss *one*, not miss touching *each* who
gathers here with what You have to give them."

At that time I could pray through the entire congregation
by name. In fact, I had the names on cards and would lay
each one on a chair (not necessarily where the person sat)
and pray for each one. Today, more than 35 years later,
though no longer with a set of name cards, it is still the
practice of our leaders to pray through the building every
Saturday, inviting the Living God to once again move

among us, touch every heart and meet every need. One of
my songs expresses this hunger:

> Let the touch of Your life, and the life of Your touch
> > Rest upon all who come within this place.
> Let the truth of Your love, and the love of Your truth
> > Fill us all as You fill us with Your grace.

Yet another,

> Here we are once again, in this place before You;
> Here we are once again, come to praise and adore You.
> > Let Your presence fill our praise,
> > Pour Your love through our hands
> As we reach to You—as we worship You, Blessed Lord.

J.W.H.

In prayer at these times, I have asked the Lord how I can
help draw each person out. I know that if that person can be
graciously led to begin to participate actively in worship, it
will eventually bring breakthrough—not only in the individual worshiper's life, but to his or her family and broader
circle of influence as well. It becomes clear that as first one,
then two or three, and then others in the congregation are
set free in worship, the whole body of a congregation will
begin "streaming to the goodness of the LORD" (Jeremiah
31:12).

Leading a congregation in worship is not a matter of a
moment's inspiration. It begins with the recognition that
people come to church with their preoccupations, worries
and hassles. Further, I am persuaded that there are hellish
emissaries whose single assignment is to extend hell's
confusion and pandemonium in Christian homes on
Sunday morning—to try to keep the people of God away,
or at least to arrive at church with a sense of frustration or

division born of the preceding two hours' stress of getting up, getting ready and getting there.

Count on this: At least ten percent of the people you lead who arrive for a Sunday service will have arrived after facing some struggle or distraction—that day! We need to meet people where they are and, with sensitivity and shepherding love, lead them into what they need—to lead them ultimately to that for which they have come like hungering sheep, oft-wearied by days of being pursued by our common adversary. People want to worship God or they wouldn't be at church. They need to meet Him, even if they doubt they deserve to—and He wants to meet them, too! And you and I, as their leaders, are the intermediaries given to pray and pave the way before we ever gather; to love and lead the flock when they arrive; to help them connect in such a way that they become willing—and thereby have gained in spiritual weight and wealth for having been at worship.

Thy Kingdom Come

It was another Saturday night and another time of praying through the sanctuary. As I paced slowly through every aisle of chairs, lightly laying my hand on the back of each seat, I captured a picture of the Savior—something like John's depiction of Him in Revelation 19, riding on a white horse. The passage declares an ultimate day when He shall come and be announced globally as King of kings and Lord of lords!

But my sense was for the moment; a sense that Jesus was ready to ride *here—tomorrow!* No words were spoken to my spirit, but the picture of Christ the Conqueror, riding a mighty stallion, rearing up with a readiness to charge, captivated my soul. And in that moment a song sprang up from my heart. It summarized my desire for the coming day's services, just as it speaks ongoingly to my quest for His manifest presence among us.

All I have offered of my thoughts to leaders, with regard to our leadership governing services in such a way that they are decently in order, is not written here to suggest I own the final word of counsel concerning anything. But I have learned a few things and submit them unto our use in the hope that any resultant benefit to you will manifest in your praying what my song cried out for, and in your congregation's experiencing His gracious gift of a full-dimensioned answer:

> Your Kingdom come! Your Kingdom come!
> In Jesus' mighty Name, Your Kingdom come!
>   O God above all time and space,
>   In power come and fill this place,
>   With great forgiveness, love and grace:
> Your Kingdom come!
>
>   J.W.H.

CHAPTER 18

A Meeting at His Throne

The Finale of Worship

Few believers will know the name of Harold Jefferies—a pastor who, through more than seventy years of leadership, was a model of influencing unity in the Church, for the most part from the base of his pastorate at the Portland, Oregon, Foursquare Church.

Harold and his wife, Ione, became unusually respected and widely received throughout the whole of the evangelical community at a time when any Pentecostal leader was liable to accusations of being at least in gross error and at worst satanic. Harold's leadership established a benchmark for church unity when he opened the way to citywide cooperation in 1950, a time when Billy Graham's earliest crusades were just beginning to realize global impact. Harold was a frequent speaker at Asian pastors' conferences under the auspices of World Vision, paving the way for the removal of obstacles that blocked a mutual trust between leaders of Baptistic and Bible Church tradition and those of classical Pentecostal and charismatic fellowship.

Unforgettable to me are the words from a message he brought to his own denomination's annual convention in the 1970s. He had taken his text from Acts 2:1–4—a predictable passage for a Pentecostal's sermon. But his remarks on that text stick in my mind to this day—filled with hope and anticipation that his expectancy might have been a prophecy we will see realized in our time.

"There is a sequence the text notes," he said. "It begins by saying first, 'They were all in one place...' together, in prayer and worship before the Lord. Second, it says they 'were all in one accord...'—united in their openness to God's presence and power. Third, it describes how 'suddenly from heaven' the Holy Spirit was poured out upon them."

As I relay his next words, let me remind you that this message was brought in the mid-1970s. "I am impressed with this sequence," Harold continued. "I am very, very moved as many of you are—touched deeply by what God is doing in the Church around the world; overflowing hosts of His own people with a revival of the Holy Spirit's power, *regardless* of any denomination, differing doctrines or historic traditions.

"In light of that fact, I am wondering about a possibility. Is it possible that, in our time, we might be experiencing the beginning of a *reverse* sequence of these three things— that at the end of Church history a cycle might be completed as we move *back through* those qualities of spiritual breakthrough that began it?

"A *reverse* sequence would look like this: First, just as the power of the Spirit was poured out upon them, we are witnessing an outpouring of His power in much the same way, as the Spirit is moving so wonderfully throughout the whole Church today, across the face of the earth.

"Second, just as they were brought into one accord as they sought the Lord in prayer and worship—could it be that the Spirit's present beginnings of renewing worship today might be the means of drawing the Church to a new unity? Into 'one accord' as increasingly, believers are joining in a new way to praise and honor God? And if that is the case, please notice the final thing in this *reverse* sequence: 'They were all in one place.'"

With that, Harold became especially animated. "I wonder," he said, "if we are just about to experience that; if this *move* of a global outpouring of the Holy Spirit and this rising *movement* toward deeper unity through worship are not a signal to us all that *we're all about to be brought to ONE PLACE*—about to hear the trumpet calling us all into God's presence at the coming of our Lord Jesus Christ!"

How well I remember my heart leaping with a sense of the Holy Spirit's desire for something of such a vision to fill the Church everywhere! Not, of course, that everyone would agree with Harold's reverse sequence idea, but that each believer would be open to the Spirit's call to do more than move upon us separately—more than to renew us in worship separately.

ONE SMALL EFFORT

Harold Jefferies was a model of Spirit-sought, loving unity among Christ's Body. His appropriately worthy welcome beyond his own denomination into such broad circles of the Church prompted me to make a request of him. My wife and I were attending a pastors' conference at which Pastor and Mrs. Jefferies were ministering about the same time as he brought the message I have quoted above.

"Dr. Jefferies," I asked, "Anna and I would like to have a brief, private moment with you and Mrs. Jefferies before the conference concludes." His gracious acknowledgment of us as younger, rising leaders in our fellowship of churches had led us to believe correctly that he would not consider this an imposition. "We simply want to have you lay your hands on us and pray for our future ministry," I explained.

The next day what took place was a time that was, for me, infused with an Elisha-like request of God that the mantle of "openness to and acceptance within Christ's Body," which Dr. Jefferies had, might be imparted to me. Though I did not specifically ask that, except in my private prayer to the Lord at that time, I was privileged later to relate to him the heartfelt hope I held at the time we prayed. He was past ninety years of age, and God's grace upon my own life—as one who was welcome across most institutional and ecclesiastical lines in the Church—was known to him. It was a touching moment because it allowed me to honor the man who had so influenced me by modeling such a servant and ministering mind-set toward the Church.

THE KING'S AUTUMN LEADERSHIP CONFERENCE

Through the years, by means of one event I frame annually and have led for more than thirty years, we have leveraged a small effort at demonstrating our pursuit of the possibility that the Church can meet, agree and function in powerful fellowship when we choose to convene *at Jesus' feet in worship*. The King's Autumn Leadership Conference has provided an opportunity for pastors and leaders from every part of the Church to gather *for* worship, to grow *in* worship and to link practical, biblical truth *to* worship. Monday to Wednesday of the second week of each November has witnessed a demonstration of Christlike unity, Christ-honoring worship and Christ-focused discipling for leadership in His Church.

I mention the Autumn Leadership Conference because it permits an illustration—the presenting of one small picture of the trust and unity that can occur when Psalm 133:1–3 becomes incarnated among us:

> Behold, how good and how pleasant it is
> For brethren to dwell together in unity!
> It is like the precious oil upon the head,
> Running down on the beard,
> The beard of Aaron,
> Running down on the edge of his garments....
> For there the LORD commanded the blessing—
> Life forevermore!

If I were to show you a list of the men and women who have accepted my invitation to speak at our conference, you would see reflected there many varied sectors in the North American Body of Christ; few would ever expect them to come to the same venue. They do, however, and I believe that each one makes the strong contribution he or she does—greatly enriching the widely mixed gathering that is present—for three reasons:

1. There is a bond of trust between each one and myself. Knowing our distinctives and differences, we trust one another, and they are readily willing to partner with me in ministering to others.

2. They believe they are not being asked to be other than themselves, to reflect other than their own convictions or to suggest they are endorsing any or every other ministry or person represented. In short, each speaker is welcomed to be what Christ has made him or her.
3. All understand we are gathering around the throne of God to worship, and around the Word of God to study; that the Holy Spirit is welcomed, but that we are not an "anything goes" band of foolhardy fanatics.

You would likely identify some of your favorite speakers and leaders in the larger Church of our Lord Jesus among the conference participants. I can tell you that the list constitutes many of mine. (I haven't yet been able to invite everyone, but neither have I ever been turned down for other than practical reasons of scheduling—never because of "differences.")

As our study together on these pages begins to draw to a conclusion, I want to underscore my passion that *the whole Church come together in worship NOW*. In light of the fact that we shall all ultimately do that—worship Him as *one body*—my heart yearns for an increase of that work of the Holy Spirit among us today. But please understand: I know that a far larger heart yearns for this, and we are wise-in-worship if we hear His heartbeat and seek to pace our pursuits to its tempo.

AN AGE-LONG HEART-CRY

The prayer began on the lips of the Church's Founder, uttered with passion on the eve before He was crucified: "Father, I pray that they may be one...." In John 17, Jesus spoke those words *five times*! And notwithstanding His age-long heart-cry, a relentless insistence abounds throughout the Church—

> ...insisting on precise liturgical requirements (that ultimately divide)
>
> ...pressing nuances of doctrinal opinion (that ultimately divide)
>
> ...rehearsing ancient arguments against brothers (that ultimately divide)
>
> ...criticizing various worship and ministry styles (that ultimately divide)

—all the while verifying our sense of some superior righteousness of view or purer refinement of God's exact ways. And while this goes on, we seem remarkably capable of not only refusing to "seek peace and pursue it" as the Bible summons (1 Peter 3:11), but also insisting that our wrestling against one another is somehow an actual exercise in righteousness!

The only way the ludicrous nature of this in-fighting or self-justified passive separatism finds logic, by which to sustain its continuance, is rooted in two foolish propositions. Humility and eventual unity are within reach if you and I are willing to acknowledge the following:

- The folly of believing that *anyone* or *any group* holds the ultimate and conclusively perfect understanding of *all* God's Word and *all* God's ways, notwithstanding His "heads-up" reminder to us that in the final analysis, His thoughts will always transcend our best, and His ways will always exceed our most sincere: " 'For My thoughts are not your thoughts, nor are your ways

My ways,' says the LORD. 'For as the heavens are higher than the earth, so are My ways higher than your ways, and My thoughts than your thoughts'" (Isaiah 55:8–9).

- The folly of believing that any invitation to or any realization of some expression of manifest unity among all believers in Jesus Christ requires a concession of private convictions or a convergence of doctrinal positions, liturgical practices or uniformity in style, ministry or emphasis. *The Bible doesn't ever require that!* The biblical grounds for unity are neither conformity nor uniformity; they are proposed on the basis of willingness to permit the Holy Spirit to bring us together at the only place we can agree—*at the feet of Jesus*:

  - where we all agree to and submit to His Lordship;
  - where we all are fixated on His worthiness rather than our own;
  - where we all might be rinsed of any residue of self-righteousness; and
  - where we all embrace Him as the Truth, more than our personal beliefs.

Contrary to those propositions that are commonly argued (whether publicly, privately or internally, as thought patterns to which we so often concede) Ephesians 4:13–16 targets our "unity of the faith" as focused in knowing Jesus and speaking the truth in love. Indeed, the passage warns against deceitful men and tricky winds of doctrinal error: The Scriptures are not neglectful to warn against both. But at some point, honest and humble souls will come to acknowledge that Christ Himself is more important than any of our systems or circles of fellowship. And that honesty and humility will bring us together, *not* into a humanly constructed institutional structure or even to the embrace of a detailed creed—but will bring us to *worship Jesus Christ— together.*

We might be prodded by the wisdom of Elton Trueblood, the beloved Quaker theologian and founder of Yokefellows, an interdenominational rallying point for believers. Trueblood said: "He who begins with loving his own view of truth more than the truth itself, will end in loving his own denomination more than Christ, and ultimately in loving himself most of all."

A Passion for Fullness

In my book of the above title, written more than fifteen years ago, I expressed much of the passion that compels my concluding this book as I am now. Mindful that "the whole body [of Christ], joined and knit together ... causes growth of the body for the edifying of itself in love" (Ephesians 4:16), it is not only clear in Scripture, but mandated of all Jesus' disciples that we commit to one another on the basis of our choice to love, not our position on truth.

This proposes no cavalier attitude toward ethics or morals, and I carry no brief for simply bypassing an expected commitment to (a) God's Word as final and authoritative, and (b) Jesus Christ as the only Savior of humankind—verified by His atoning death on the cross, His literal resurrection and His glorious ascension to the Father's right hand as exalted Lord of the Church. That is enough to bring us into His presence to worship—together; to worship as one with God's Word as our foundation of faith and God's Son as the Chief Cornerstone of His

Church, which He longs to see "built together for a dwelling place of God in the Spirit" (Ephesians 2:22).

To separate myself, when such grounds as these furnish a kneeling place beside you—focused upon Him and worshiping in His presence—is to yield to a sinister, self-justifying spirit of religious legalism and its inevitable pharisaical will to brutalize Christ's Body rather than submit to His larger-than-my-system call.

But I believe increasing millions of believers who call Jesus their Savior and are being discipled in His Word are ready to answer a dual call—to *worship* and to worship *together*.

MOVEMENT TOWARD THE FINALE

Harold Jefferies' perception of the unity found among the earliest believers and how it was secured and readied for the Church to be born "as one" is so worthwhile. Their unity was begotten as that band of 120 knelt in prayer and discovered the bonding power of bowing in worship before the throne of God—to which they had just witnessed their Lord's ascension. Harold's linking of today's globe-sweeping increase of the Holy Spirit's working, joined to an increase in the Church's willingness to open to the Holy Spirit's call to worship, is equally significant. And with the stunning, awesome and oft-overwhelming evidences that ours could be the days of earth's finale, we are left with every reason to expect that heaven's blast of the last trumpet may be about to sound.

> Therefore, since all these things will be dissolved, what manner of persons ought you to be in holy conduct and godliness, looking for and hastening the coming of the day of God?
>
> 2 Peter 3:11–12

These words of the Spirit issue a timely point of conclusion for our study together. We are being called to *more* than worship—we are being called to let our worship shape us unto a "manner of persons" who are willing to be bonded together in the presence of God and to become banded together for the extending of His Kingdom. Until that day, let us chorus together:

> O how we yearn, come back again; Jesus return, Savior of men.
> Tho' we rejoice now in Your power, longing we pray for that hour.
> Trumpets will sound, clouds roll away, then every eye shall behold You.
> Until that day, ever we'll sing, "Lord Jesus, come and be King."[1]

---

[1] "Come and Be King" by Jack W. Hayford. Copyright © 1981 by Annamarie Music. ASCAP. All rights reserved.

Appendix 1

A Prayer for Receiving Christ as Lord and Savior

It seems possible that some earnest inquirer may have read this book and somehow still never have received Jesus Christ as personal Savior. If this is true of you—if you have never personally welcomed the Lord Jesus into your heart to be your Savior and to lead you in the matters of your life—I would like to encourage you and help you to do that.

There is no need to delay, for an honest heart can approach the loving Father God at any time. So I would like to invite you to come with me. Let's pray to Him right now.

If it is possible there where you are, bow your head, or even kneel if you can. In either case, let me pray a simple prayer first, and then I have added words for you to pray yourself.

MY PRAYER

Father God, I have the privilege of joining with this child of Yours who is reading this book right now. I want to thank You for the openness of heart being shown toward You and I want to praise You for Your promise that when we call to You, You will answer.

I know that genuine sincerity is present in this heart, which is ready to speak this prayer, and so we come to You in the name and through the cross of Your Son, the Lord Jesus. Thank You for hearing.

And now, speak your prayer.

YOUR PRAYER

Dear God, I am doing this because I believe in Your love for me, and I want to ask You to come to me as I come to You. Please help me now.

First, I thank You for sending Your Son, Jesus, to earth to live and to die for me on the cross. I thank You for the gift of forgiveness of sin that You offer me now, and I pray for that forgiveness.

Forgive me and cleanse my life in Your sight through the blood of Jesus Christ. I am sorry for anything and everything I have ever done that is unworthy in Your sight. Please take away all guilt and shame, as I accept the facts that Jesus died to pay for all my sins and that through Him I am now given forgiveness on this earth and eternal life in heaven.

I ask You, Lord Jesus, please come into my life now. Because You rose from the dead, I know You're alive, and I want You to live with me—now and forever.

I am turning my life over to You and from my way to Yours. I invite Your Holy Spirit to fill me and lead me forward in a life that will please the heavenly Father.

Thank You for hearing me. From this day forward, I commit myself to Jesus Christ, the Son of God. In His name. Amen.[1]

[1] From *The Anatomy of Seduction* by Jack W. Hayford, p. 111. Copyright © 2004 by Regal Books, Ventura, CA 93003. Used by permission.

APPENDIX 2

A Prayer for Inviting the Lord to Fill You with the Holy Spirit

Dear Lord Jesus,
I thank You and praise You for Your great love and faithfulness to me.

My heart is filled with joy whenever I think of the great gift of salvation You have given to me so freely.

And I humbly glorify You, Lord Jesus, for You have forgiven me all my sins and brought me to the Father.

Now I come in obedience to Your call.

I want to receive the fullness of the Holy Spirit.

I do not come because I am worthy myself, but because You have invited me to come.

Because You have washed me from my sins, I thank You that You have made the vessel of my life a worthy one to be filled with the Holy Spirit of God.

I want to be overflowed with Your life, Your love and Your power, Lord Jesus.

I want to show forth Your grace, Your words, Your goodness and Your gifts to everyone I can.

And so, with simple, childlike faith, I ask You, Lord, to fill me with the Holy Spirit. I open all of myself to You to receive all of Yourself in me.

I love You, Lord, and I lift my voice in praise to You.

I welcome Your might and Your miracles to be manifested in me, for Your glory and unto Your praise.[1]

I am not asking you to say "Amen" at the end of this prayer because after inviting Jesus to fill you, it is good to begin to praise Him in faith. Praise and worship Jesus, simply allowing the Holy Spirit to help you do so. He will manifest Himself in a Christ-glorifying way, and you can ask Him to enrich this moment by causing you to know the presence and power of the Lord Jesus.

Don't hesitate to expect the same things in your experience as occurred to people in the Bible. The spirit of praise is an appropriate way to express that expectation. And to make Jesus your focus, worship as you praise. Glorify Him and leave the rest to the Holy Spirit.

---

[1]. From *The Anatomy of Seduction* by Jack W. Hayford, p. 113. Copyright © 2004 by Regal Books, Ventura, CA 93003. Used by permission.

INDEX

Jack W. Hayford is founding pastor of The Church On The Way in Van Nuys, California, president of the International Church of the Foursquare Gospel and chancellor of The King's College and Seminary in Los Angeles. He is also founder of the Jack W. Hayford School of Pastoral Nurture—a ministry that has had an impact on thousands of pastors from more than sixty denominations and numerous independent groups. He speaks to more than twenty thousand Church leaders annually and has ministered in more than sixty nations. Jack has also written more than forty books and composed nearly six hundred hymns and choruses, including the internationally known "Majesty." His radio and television ministry has extended throughout the U.S. and in most parts of the world. He serves on numerous boards of Christian ministries and agencies.

Jack and his wife, Anna (she, too, is a licensed minister), have been married for fifty years, having united while in their junior year of college. They entered public ministry beginning as youth ministers in 1956 and have served together in pastoral ministry as well as in fields of education. They are both graduates of LIFE Bible College in Los Angeles. Jack also graduated from Azusa Pacific University, which in 1998 designated him alumnus of the year.

Additional information may be found by contacting:

The King's College and Seminary
14800 Sherman Way
Van Nuys, California 91405

www.kingsseminary.edu
www.jackhayford.org